Edward Lee Hicks

Traces of Greek Philosophy and Roman Law in the New Testament

Edward Lee Hicks

Traces of Greek Philosophy and Roman Law in the New Testament

ISBN/EAN: 9783744773249

Printed in Europe, USA, Canada, Australia, Japan

Cover: Foto ©Thomas Meinert / pixelio.de

More available books at **www.hansebooks.com**

TRACES

OF

GREEK PHILOSOPHY AND ROMAN LAW

IN THE

NEW TESTAMENT.

BY

EDWARD HICKS, D.D., D.C.L.,
VICAR OF ST. STEPHEN'S, SHEFFIELD.

PUBLISHED UNDER THE DIRECTION OF THE TRACT COMMITTEE.

LONDON:
SOCIETY FOR PROMOTING CHRISTIAN KNOWLEDGE,
NORTHUMBERLAND AVENUE, W.C.; 43, QUEEN VICTORIA STREET, E.C.
BRIGHTON: 129, NORTH STREET.
NEW YORK: E. & J. B. YOUNG & CO.
1896.

PREFACE.

THE work here presented is but a sketch. When first written, the idea of publishing was not entertained. It was an essay offered for the degree of D.D. in the University of Durham. The Professor of Divinity, in adjudicating upon it, deemed it worthy of publication, either in whole or in part, and urged the usefulness of such a course.

The title will show that the range of subject is limited both in scope and time. The brief work treats only of two questions, and it relates to the Church history of the first century. It is an attempt to show the probable influence, in character and extent, of Greek philosophy and Roman law on the minds of the New Testament writers; the contribution made by each to the doctrinal thought, or to its formal expression in language; and to exhibit how, in a general way as well as in closer detail, the Gospel was thus assisted in its proclamation amongst mankind. The subject deserves and demands closer and more extended study, to which these pages may, I hope, act as an incentive.

It may be permitted to say that in speculating concerning religion, as well as in science, each hypothesis suggested ought not only to be *adaequata*, i. e. sufficient to explain the phenomena which are under investigation, but also *vera*, i. e. not only a real fact in Nature, but a fact which can be proved to have relation to the special point. If the former condition be met, while the latter is neglected, the hypothesis is a possibility; not a probability; still less a certainty.

My desire has been to exhibit the scope and force of Greek philosophy and of Roman law; not speculating vaguely on their possible influence, but estimating their effects according to the weight which evidence and historic fact offer. With the projection into the New Testament narratives of pagan legendary miracle or of heathen folk-lore, as asserted by some, I have nothing here to do. I will only say that with the attempts which have been made to trace Christian institutions to a heathen source or mythological origin, e. g. to the Eleusinian mysteries, or, again, to assign the idea of a virgin birth to mythology, I am wholly out of sympathy.

The last great fact stands apart, on its own basis of evidence and Divine probability, unaffected by Philonean allegorizing or Greek and Egyptian fable. The same is true as regards the integrant conceptions of Christian Theology. The inquiry I have followed, and the line of thought taken, are in a different plane.

I trust that that modesty which is demanded by Theology, as by all sciences, at the hands of inquirers, will not be found to be overstepped in the following pages; and that the reverence due to the inspired Scriptures has nowhere been forgotten.

The first division of our subject, that devoted to the Greek philosophy, is necessarily the larger in bulk, as touching a much wider literature and running in more extended and less direct avenues. The authorities consulted in this portion are, of course, open to all. I have, I hope, duly expressed acknowledgements wherever necessary. In the second portion, which has been to me, I confess, the more interesting, as allowing of more definite treatment, and touching, for the most part, untrodden ground, authorities, after works of a strictly legal character, are not so easily found. I am indebted to some extent to Dr. W. E. Ball, whose article in the *Contemporary* for August, 1891, though only seen two years after the completion of this portion of my work, has suggested additional thoughts by its felicitous language. Also to Dr. Curwen, Rector of Plumbland, Carlisle, for some thoughts in an essay presented for his degree of D.C.L. in the University of Durham. His explanation by means of the Praetorian Will (see p. 158) of a passage in the Revelation of St. John (v. 1), may rank as an exegetical discovery.

E. H.

March, 1896.

CONTENTS.

	PAGE
PREFACE	3
I. INTRODUCTION	9

GREEK PHILOSOPHY.

SPECULATIVE PHILOSOPHY.

II. PLATONISM	15
III. ALEXANDRIA AND PHILO	29
IV. THE LOGOS IN THE NEW TESTAMENT	49
V. KINDRED TRACES. THE EPISTLE TO THE HEBREWS, ETC.	65

ETHICAL PHILOSOPHY.

VI. THE FOUR SCHOOLS	91
VII. ETHICAL TRACES	101

ROMAN LAW.

		PAGE
VIII.	ROMAN LAW AT THE CHRISTIAN ERA . .	123
IX.	ROMAN LAW AND THE PROGRESS OF THE EARLY CHURCH	135
X.	ALLUSIONS TO ROMAN LAW IN THE NEW TESTAMENT	151
XI.	ROMAN LAW IN ST. PAUL'S EPISTLES . .	161
XII.	NOTE ON THE TERMS "ADOPTION" AND "REGENERATION"	186

TRACES OF GREEK PHILOSOPHY AND ROMAN LAW IN THE NEW TESTAMENT.

I.

INTRODUCTION.

THE world may be said, at the Christian era, to have exhausted itself in its efforts after truth and the final knowledge of things. It had "sought after God." But its golden age of philosophy was past. Alexandria, the university of the world, sheltered in its halls the ancient faith of Israel and the thought of Greece, mingled with the mystical wisdom of the Orientals. Rome, which had become a centre of intellectual exertion, had been examining with eagerness the treasures, found through her material conquests, in the writings of Plato and Aristotle and their successors. But invention in thought was at a standstill. Eclecticism prevailed. Thought was settling down into a kind of indifferentism, under the burden of its accumulated learning. Scepticism, the latest legacy of the academies, one in its aim as a practical philosophy of life with Stoicism and its apathy, and with Epicureanism, "the philosophy of the careless," exhibited also the same want of originality. Men's minds were looking backward, not forward. They were gathering up the fragments of the old, and elaborating and combining as they could the ideas contained in previous systems. An age of mighty intellectual energy had moved, and wrought, and subsided, and still "the world by wisdom knew not God."

Religiously, morally, and intellectually, it was the time of the world's need. The old faiths of heathenism were crumbling away as the mythical elements of which they were composed were melting in the critical light that philosophy and its methods had thrown upon them. The monotheism of the Jews was embracing some of the nobler of the conceptions with which it had come into contact in Platonism and Greek thought. And yet at the same time the morality of the age was growing corrupt in the frivolous unreality of sceptical sophistry and general unbelief. The world seemed waiting for some catastrophe or some enlightenment that should bring what was new and pure and saving to the rescue of the decaying old.

In such an age the Gospel was revealed. The books of the New Testament are the work of one generation, but of various men strongly moved by the power which morally renovated them and spiritually enlightened them; and their message, for so it distinctly professed to be, found ready to its service a sea of language and of mental ideas, which, mingling in the haven of Alexandria, and from thence carried by many a tide and in many a stream, became a highway upon which were borne to men's acceptance the greater realities which the Gospel offered.

Philosophy had bequeathed a language. Alexandria was the home, not only of a new mode of thought, as seen in Philo's system, if such it may be called, but of a new repertory of words and ideas which supplied a current coin for the exchange of every kind of mental conception. As the Hebrew Scriptures and the Greek dialectic met, and formed a new philosophy, so this philosophy supplied new terms of thought. Even the strangely mingled, fantastic theology of Gnosticism, which was to trouble and hinder the Divine truth, was already pressed into the service of the eternal faith, and forced to lend its terms to a truer Gnosis.

"Alexandrianism," it has been well said, "was not the seed of the great tree which was to cover the earth, but the soil in which it grew up. It was not the body of which Christianity was the soul, but the vesture in which it folded itself. It was a literature, not a life." It was the connecting link by means of which Christianity was enabled to reach the minds of those who thought as Greeks as well as Jews. And thus the traces which we find in the New Testament of Greek philosophy are less often direct than indirect, more often perhaps unconscious than designed; and where religion and philosophy meet through the medium of language, language is elevated to a higher meaning and a vaster service, and religion begins to form an idiom of its own.

Nor in Alexandria alone were such influences at work. In a lesser degree, and in another way, Tarsus, the birthplace of St. Paul, contributed its share. As a seat of Greek learning, Tarsus held an important and leading place; and of all the schools, Stoicism, to the language of which there are some striking parallels in the New Testament, was the most ably represented. If Stoicism had its birthplace in the East, Tarsus was a "half-way house" for the philosophy which matured in the West. For again, it was among the Romans that Stoicism was most earnestly received, and achieved its greatest influence. And thus, throughout the then world of thought and civilization, the elements of philosophy and the seeds of thought were scattered, and were growing into a harvest which was to be reaped by the all-embracing spirit of Christianity.

Nor, again, were the secular events of the age otherwise than conducive to the general preparation for and reception of the new message. The Roman power, while it opened the roads and markets of the world to wide and peaceful intercourse, protected and educated it at the same time by its mighty legal system, the greatest and most perfect in its form and logic that the world has ever known. And the dominance of a race possessing this element of mental leadership was one more contributory factor to the progress of the revelation of Jesus Christ. And as the Gospel made its way along the Roman roads and into the Roman cities and colonies everywhere established, its foremost pioneer and apostle was himself not only a deeply religious Jew, a disciple of Gamaliel and a cultivated man of the religious world, but at the same time a free-born Roman citizen, conversant with the principles and language of a jurisprudence which could not fail to be of help to him as he preached to Roman and Greek and Jew, by its marvellous adaptiveness to the thoughts and conceptions of a theology which he was to do so much to formulate.

In the writings of the New Testament, accordingly, which came to men as pointing out the fulfilment of what was permanent and eternal in the Hebrew faith, we find distinct traces also of Greek philosophy and of Roman law. If for the need, so also much more for the supply of that need, it was for the world "the fullness of time;" and the message which spoke from the cross of the Redeemer was "written in Hebrew, and in Latin, and in Greek." "These three languages gathered up the results of the religious, the social, the intellectual preparation for Christ, and, in each, witness was given to His office [1]."

And so the title which the Roman governor placed there, and declined to remove, was an unconscious assertion and prophecy not only of the Divine royalty of the Victim, but also of the world-wide meaning of His life and death, taking place as it did in that focus of the world of Jew, and Roman, and Greek.

[1] Westcott, *Gospel of St. John*, Introd.

SPECULATIVE PHILOSOPHY.

II.

The Greek Philosophy. Platonism.

The four chief schools, of Plato, Aristotle, Zeno, and Epicurus, had become established as the recognized philosophical systems. But the older pre-Socratic doctrines were resuscitated, not always consciously, by the professional interpreters of philosophy, and in the hands of the syncretists a general harmonization and assimilation was elaborated. Thus, the old philosophy of Heraclitus, of Pythagoras, of Parmenides, all of them more or less assimilated by Plato, as well as the later methods of the Cynics and the Sceptics, were brought forward. Alexandria and Rome, no longer Athens, had become the theatre of philosophical development; and to the Roman the forms which were most attractive were the more ethical and less speculative systems of Epicurus and Zeno.

Thus the New Testament was more indebted

to the general influence and language of philosophy, and to the strange infusion of various elements which we have already indicated as existing at Alexandria, than to any special form of power which philosophy possessed in the apostles' days.

Accordingly, we must not look in the Christian Scriptures for any adoption into its system of truth, or acceptance in any recognized form, of "the wisdom of this world" which it emphatically repudiated. Yet at the same time, just as in the present day there is always a floating terminology, arising from the passing condition of science or thought, as well as a freer, social "cant" of the every-day world, so that the sermons of divines no less than the writings of thinkers, poets, and fictionists, abound in terms which give point and form to their utterances, whether they accept the passing philosophy or not; so in the days of the apostles of Christianity, only to greater purpose and more permanent value, the ideas of the age, expressed in words and phrases, were a power not to be left out of account, and which it would have been unnatural if not impossible to refrain from using to help forward the great truth for which the way had already thus been prepared.

For, if the Almighty speaks indeed to mankind, He can but speak to men in their own tongue. If the Incarnation of the Son was necessary that men might learn the Father, this was but the carrying out on the vaster scale what was also being done through stammering lips and strange tongues as men conversed with one another on the earth. The truth and miracle of inspiration is seen in its taking the thoughts and words of men as men could best receive them, in order to convey to them its own transcendent message, much more than in any ideal revelation which should speak a language entirely its own, and therefore uncomprehended on earth. There is, and must be, a link always between the revealer and the recipients of truth, or revelation is impossible; and we are thinking artificially, we are assuming a situation which cannot be said to exist, when we isolate Christianity from all that surrounds or preceded it, and thus preclude the interpretative help of language as commonly received among men. That which differentiates Christianity from everything earthly is its essence, its spirit, its direct, Divine message. That which unites it with and makes possible its reception in the world is its outer habiliment, its vehicle, its method of speech. And the sequence of thought from age to age; the forms of spiritual conception, even of speculation, which have obtained among men; become the servant, the handmaid of the Truth; a new power breathes in old thought; "language dead for ages awakens into life."

A better proof and example of this cannot be given than the history of the philosophico-religious term Logos.

The two courses which it ran—philosophical and theological,—as Reason and as Word—as the expression of a Greek and a Hebrew thought, are deeply interesting to trace.

The Greek mind saw the world as a κόσμος, produced, therefore, and ruled by a reasoning principle, or λόγος. From Heraclitus to the Stoics, from the Stoics to Philo Judaeus, the term passed; changed, modified, expanded in turns, but always there.

With Heraclitus, the "weeping philosopher," who saw all things in a perpetual flux, and fire as their origin and end, the λόγος was really inseparable from the world. In man it is the soul. It is the relation or reason of things, objectively. In no sense is it speech or word. In the constant conflict between opposites, in the process towards orderly relation, the λόγος is the principle upon which this takes place—shall we say, in modern phrase, "Natural Law"?

With Anaxagoras came in the doctrine of a ruling νοῦς, or supreme intelligent principle.

In Plato and Aristotle the term λόγος appears, but subordinately; a term of many senses, inferior to the νοῦς, which divinely rules. Nevertheless, the Ideas of Plato, the λόγος and the λόγοι, are not far from absorption into the mind of the Eternal.

The Stoics brought the word more forward. The λόγος is the active principle which lives in and determines the world, and is even called God, though conceived of as material. It is the operative principle. The λόγος σπερματικός is the world-law of generation, reason working in dead matter. Then the λόγοι σπερματικοί, distributed through the universe, resembling the λόγοι ἔνυλοι of Aristotle, omit not man, who possesses his special λόγος, which, as his bosom thought, is ἐνδιάθετος, as his spoken word προφορικός, the λόγος as *ratio*, and the λόγος as *oratio*; or Aristotle's ἔξω λόγος and λόγος ἐν τῇ ψυχῇ.

At length, arriving at Philo, the religionist, the eclectic, the syncretist, we find the thoughts and terms of Platonism and Stoicism mingled with the truths of the Old Testament, or rather, worked in with its language, so as to form a new philosophy.

We find much of the λόγος. In the world it is the archetypal λόγος, the Idea, and appears in the λόγοι or rational germs of material things. It looks not only from God to man, but from man to God. It has a new sense; it is now an Alexandrian term.

But we now proceed more fully to dwell upon the process by which the two courses, the philosophical and the theological, became mingled, and the Hellenic and the Hebrew characteristics of the λόγος blended in one; and to trace moreover other influences of the old philosophies, which, passing through Alexandria, had their part in forming Christian thought or in supplying a Christian terminology.

The limits of our subject confine us to the New Testament and its debt to the philosophy of ancient Greece. A little further down, in and beyond the second century, the task would be an easy one to trace the thoughts and influences, especially of Platonism, on the minds and in the writings of Christian theologians; but to pronounce how far many an apparent resemblance in the writings of the apostles to the utterances of heathen thought are traceable to that source, or in any way certainly connected, is a matter of no small difficulty. Much must ever remain uncertain.

It was Alexandrian Platonism that, most of all, represented the ancient Greek philosophy as coming in contact with Christianity; and it is through the philosophical language of Philo Judaeus that the New Testament was enabled to meet and to cope with the quickly rising Gnosticism which had its origin on the one hand in Alexandrianism itself, and in Orientalism on the other, in the strangely mingled condition of thought which then and there prevailed.

Yet, indirectly, perhaps the stern truthfulness of Aristotle, his lofty ethics, his notion of conscience, the idea of citizenship that proclaims its rights over the individual, reproduced again in the Stoic Seneca, contributed to much of the moral thought that was a ready soil for the New Testament teaching. The ground was preparing for the higher Truth, which was to be "made manifest in men's consciences [1]."

And on the other hand, the direct, material, practical individualism of the later teaching, belonging to an unsettled age when states were crumbling, of Zeno and Epicurus, calling upon the man as he is in himself, to think out his way and his road, was not less preparatory. The question, τί με δεῖ ποιεῖν ἵνα σωθῶ [2]; was to receive a final answer in the heavenly Message.

Yet it is the abstract philosophy of Plato that first and foremost arouses our attention in its far-reaching effects. And at the same time, the terminology that had obtained was to some extent the result of a commingling of the

[1] 2 Cor. v. 11.   [2] Acts xvi. 30.

abstractions of Platonism with the more physical notions of Stoicism.

Stoicism was an expression of philosophical Monism. As in the Ionic theory, the world consisted of a single substance. Reason and force, both inherent in matter, produced the movements and modifications of the universe. The Stoic spoke of the Active and the Passive. The Passive might be simply ὕλη, the timber from which the carpenter fashions his objects; the Active might be termed λόγος, thought or will, expressed in a sentence or shown in a law. But the Stoics came to attach personality to the latter term, and so "God" might come to be thought of as a mode of matter, as matter was by some regarded as a mode of God[1]. He might be the *natura naturata*, or the *natura naturans*. "He is always moving with purpose and system, and always thereby producing the world." The products, all Divine, are not equally so. The human soul is nearest God, and in an especial sense His offspring. Furthest from Him is matter, the atoms of which are held together by the cohesive force which is

[1] Hatch, *Hibbert Lectures*, vii. Hatch is very helpful in analyzing and setting in order the Greek philosophical conceptions; but some of his conclusions, as to the kind and extent of their effect upon Christianity, must be accepted with cautious reserve. Those conclusions do not affect us here.

still God. "If all this were expressed in modern terms, and by the help of later conceptions, it would be most suitably gathered into the proposition that the world is the self-evolution of God[1]."

Platonism, on the other hand, expressed philosophical Dualism. As Anaxagoras, so Plato too believed that mind, acting on matter, is absolutely separate from it. The real and the phenomenal stand opposed. The world was originally τὸ μὴ ὄν, only potentially existent. In forming it, the reason or mind of God was exercised, νοῦν καὶ φρόνησιν τινὰ θαυμαστήν[2]. Each thought of God is exhibited in a group of material objects, which are the embodiments of a form or pattern existent in the Divine mind, or proceeding forth from that mind to act. In the latter conception, they become cosmic forces, causes. They mediated between the unapproachable, unchanging God, and the changing phenomena of rude matter. Thus a chain of vast gradation reached from the Divine perfection to the lowest mode of being. The Demiurgus, the creative energy, made the world, ideally, and his agents performed the rest, by which it became actual. As a human artist first forms in his mind his plan of work, and then executes it by means of his servants and

---

[1] Hatch, *Hibbert Lectures*, vii.   [2] *Phileb.* 16.

labourers, so, it was conceived, did the Divine Being, in creating the universe, proceed, lower powers carrying out that which was below the dignity or possibility of the touch of Infinity [1].

We have spoken of the age of syncretism which followed the greater age of Greek philosophy. And the two great "drifts of thought" above named tended to approach each other. Stoicism, monistic, emphasized two phases of the one substance, and tended to become dualistic. Platonism, dualistic, distinguishing between the creating energy of the Divine Being and the "pattern" in the Divine mind, tended to bring into the idea of creation another and a third factor. And so a method of speech grew up which implied three principles, known as God, Matter, and Form. "Hence came in a new fusion of conceptions. The Platonic Forms in the mind of God, conceived, as they sometimes were, as causes of operating outside Him, were more or less identified with the Stoical logoi, and, being viewed as the manifold expressions of a single logos, were expressed by a singular rather than a plural term, the logos rather than the logoi of God.

"It is at this point that the writings of Philo become of special importance. They gather together, without fusing into a symmetrical

---

[1] See Seneca, *Ep. Mor.* 65. 10.

system, the two dominant theories of the past[1]."

And so, out of the eclectic thinking and the mingled phraseology of that era, grew up the Alexandrian philosophy, which has affected the language of the New Testament, and which was in brief both Judaism and Platonism; that is, a belief in a personal God, and an acceptance of the theory of Ideas.

"The ideal theory," says Archer Butler[2], "is a reaction from the eleatic theory of unity; a return from the doctrine of the absolute simplicity of the rational world to the prior Pythagorean doctrine of 'unity in multiplicity.'"

Plato believed in a world of reality, invisible to and immeasurably above the material order of things. The objects and images of the world around us, of the visible universe, are, as being fleeting and perishing, not themselves realities, but shadows only; the realities being the archetypes in the mind of the Divine, the patterns of things sensible, which patterns are permanent and eternal. Thus he reconciled "the Many and the One." "Our doctrine," he says in the *Philebus*, "is, that one and the same thing (the one common notion) which, ὑπὸ λόγων, under the influence of our thoughts and words, becomes

---

[1] Hatch, *Hibbert Lectures*, vii.
[2] *Anc. Philos.* vol. ii. p. 119.

one and many, circulates everywhere, in regard to everything of which existence is asserted from time to time."

When he describes[1] the vision which blessed the immortal souls in their voyaging to the highest heaven, without and upon the dome of the convex sky, he declares that they then saw, by the power of reason, the colourless, formless, impalpable Being. In that journey the soul's intelligence, like that of God, beheld and loved and was fed by the vision of truth, "until, in cycle, the revolving movement brings it round again to the same place. And in that journey round it beholds Justice itself; it looks upon Temperance, upon Knowledge; not in the form of created things or of things relative; but the knowledge absolute in absolute existence (τὴν ἐν τῷ ὅ ἐστιν ὂν ὄντως ἐπιστήμην οὖσαν): and having beheld, after the same manner, all other true existences, passing again to the interior of the heavens, the soul returned home."

And in this return, the soul on earth has recollections of that former blessed state, whence its ideas of the fundamentals of truth, as shown in the doctrine of reminiscences, to which we shall again refer, which is one of Plato's proofs of our immortality.

This beautiful fancy has been made familiar

[1] *Phaedrus*, 247.

to us by our own poet Wordsworth, in his "Ode on the Intimations of Immortality:"

> "Our birth is but a sleep and a forgetting:
> The Soul that rises with us, our life's Star,
>   Hath had elsewhere its setting,
>   And cometh from afar:
>   Not in entire forgetfulness,
>   And not in utter nakedness,
> But trailing clouds of glory do we come
>   From God, who is our home."

And again:

> "Though inland far we be,
> Our Souls have sight of that immortal sea
>   Which brought us hither,
>   Can in a moment travel thither,
> And see the Children sport upon the shore,
> And hear the mighty waters rolling evermore."

And does not Tennyson echo the same in his "Crossing the Bar"?

> "When that which drew from out the boundless deep
>   Turns again home."

"Hitherto, in the Socratic disputations, the ideas had been creations of our reason. With Plato, they are the creators of our reason [1]."

Here, then, is our point. What the old Platonic notion endeavoured to explain by the doctrine of reminiscences, by the theory of ultimate Ideas presented in the far-off past to the soul—what man is conscious of, and may darkly grope to understand—that, in all the

[1] Walter Pater, *Plato and Platonism*.

definiteness of revelation, is set before us in the words, "God created man in His own image [1];" "He left not Himself without witness [2];" "There was the true Light, which lighteth every man, coming into the world [3];" "That which may be known of God is manifest in them [4]."

The Platonic Ideas stood for truth; the Jew Philo, with his belief in a personal God, mingled, with the revelation of his own people, the philosophy of the Greeks; with what result we now proceed to consider.

[1] Gen. i. 27.   [2] Acts xiv. 17.   [3] John i. 9 (R. V.).
[4] Rom. i. 19.

III.

Alexandria and Philo.

The doctrine of ideas and the theology of Judaism met, and in the contact both were modified. There was produced the peculiar philosophy of Alexandria. The notions of the good, the true, the beautiful, deeply impressed the Jewish mind; and Philo, receiving and admiring the Grecian wisdom, declared that what of wisdom Socrates, Plato, or Aristotle possessed, had been derived really from Moses himself, "who at an early age attained the very summits of philosophy."

Allegorical interpretation did all that was needed to bring Greek philosophy into harmonious service with the Hebrew Scriptures. Philo produces a labyrinth of rhetoric, mysticism, and logic.

The allegorical method, which became so strong a feature of the Jewish-Alexandrian philosophy, was freely employed by the Stoics. Before them, the older philosophers had endeavoured to make the grossness of the popular mythology more presentable as well as useful to the minds of the people by showing that some profound truth or edifying principle underlay the belief or legend. The Stoics developed the system; and a work by Heraclitus on "Homeric Allegories," and one by Cornutus on "The Nature of the Gods," shows us how far they advanced; and "we find here," says Professor Drummond [1], "as an efficient instrument of interpretation, that wonderful system of etymology which was afterwards wielded with such reckless disregard of philological possibility by Philo. The soul of the universe was called Ζεύς, from ζῆν, because it lived through all and was the cause of life to the living; or κατὰ τὸ ζέον τῆς ὕλης, a derivation connected with the doctrine that Ζεύς was the pristine fire." Then it becomes Δεύς; and Δία, because δι' αὐτὸν γίνεται καὶ σώζεται τὰ πάντα (!). And so on.

Philo repeatedly refers to the four elements of the universe. He utilizes them to account for the commands of the Mosaic economy. Hence the four spices of the incense [2]. Hence also the four materials of which the Tabernacle curtains were made. The linen represented the earth out of which it grew; the hyacinth represented the (black) air; the purple stood for water, from which comes the dye of the shellfish; the scarlet resembles fire. The reason that these

[1] *Philo Judaeus*, vol. i. p. 121.   [2] *Quis rer. div. her.*, 41.

materials were selected was that they were to form a house for the Father of the universe, which therefore they must resemble [1]. The same four elements were used in the ten plagues of Egypt [2]. And so on. Further on, where he speaks of the servants of Abraham and Isaac digging four wells, so, he says, there are "in the cosmos earth and water and air and heaven, these four [3]."

In Philo's anthropology man is a duad. But he borrows the Platonic, and even the Aristotelian tripartite division, when referring, not to the composition, but the functions of the soul. Where in one passage he distributes the soul into mind, speech, and perception, he is driven into a strange confusion by allegorizing from Abraham's offering of the heifer, the ram, and the she-goat, which are made to represent the human faculties [4].

But his philosophy goes deeper than this apparently futile play upon Scripture imagery. In discussing the origin of the universe, in a dialogue with Alexander, he seems from the exigencies of the argument to adopt the hypothesis of its eternity, and appeals to the "most celebrated philosophers, Parmenides, Empe-

---

[1] *Cong. erud. gr.* 21 ; *Vita Mosis,* iii. 6.
[2] *Vita Mosis,* i. 17.   [3] *Somn.* i. 3.
[4] *De Cherub.* 32; *Leg. All.* iii. 13, &c.

docles, Zeno, Cleanthes, and other Divine men, and as it were a certain true and strictly sacred assembly."

Yet even in his deeper discussions Philo allegorizes still. On the nature of God, who, as the Cause of all things, is a genus by Himself, and the highest, he endeavours to draw truth from the account of the water and manna supplied to Israel in the wilderness. The manna is the most generic thing, for it is called " what," or the universal genus. The people said [1], "What is this [2]?" "The most generic thing [3]," Philo says, " is God, and second is the Word of God, but all other things exist in word only, and in reality are equivalent to the non-existent [4]." In this strange combination Philo is both a Jew and a philosopher.

And the Hebrew Lord of hosts and King of kings, the God ὁ ὤν, becomes also τὸ ὄν, νοητὴ φύσις, ὁ νοῦς τῶν ὄντων. Incomprehensible and invisible, the Divinity embodying the ἰδέαι of Plato is, with Philo, a Being apart, withdrawn, separated from His world.

"The most generic thing is God, and second is the logos. And the logos of God is above all the cosmos, and oldest and most generic of the things that have come into being [5]." So then

---

[1] Exodus xvi. 15.   [2] Τί ἐστι τοῦτο, LXX.
[3] Τὸ γενικώτατον.   [4] Leg. All. ii. 21.   [5] Ibid. iii. 59-61, &c.

reason or thought ranks next in order to the Eternal Being or the Divine Essence.

Thus the logos is γενικώτατος, and the δυνάμεις, by which the universe is bound together, are the invisible powers of God. In the thought of them are combined both the Platonic and the Stoic notions. They are the ἰδέαι of Plato, while they seem to be the λόγοι of Stoicism. On the Jewish side they are often taken to be the ἄγγελοι or manifestations of God given to man in the Old Testament. Thus they would be personal; and Gfrörer, and after him Jowett, appear to take them in this sense. But closer criticism and analysis of Philo's long and varied expositions of the subject may bring us to another conclusion[1]. While adopting the term "angels" in many places, the logoi or powers, which are really identical, are hardly meant to be conceived of as beings with the personality of Divine messengers in our sense of the word. They are "angels" because they are messages rather than messengers, and it is Philo's intense love of allegorizing that permits him to speak of the "immortal logoi, whom it is customary to call angels." In one of these passages Jacob, who represents the mental character which strives by self-discipline to attain wisdom and

[1] See Drummond's examination of the question, in vol. ii. ch. v. &c.

goodness (as Abraham and Isaac respectively represented Instruction and Nature), we learn that "the ascetic understanding is subject to irregular movements, going up and down continually; and, whenever it is elevated, it is illumined by the archetypal and incorporeal beams of the rational fountain of the perfect God, but whenever it descends it is lighted ' by the images of these immortal logoi, whom it is customary to call angels [1].'" But in the same allegory, the stones that formed Jacob's pillow are also, like the angels, logoi. And "Jacob, having taken one of these logoi, selecting the highest in merit, places it near his head, his understanding; for this is in a manner the head of the soul. And he does this ostensibly to sleep, but in reality to rest on a Divine logos ($\epsilon\pi\grave{\iota}$ $\lambda\acute{o}\gamma\wp$ $\theta\epsilon\acute{\iota}\wp$), and place upon that his whole life as a very light burden [2]."

This will serve to show something of Philo's style of allegorizing, and also the difficulty of being sure sometimes of his exact meaning or degree of literalness.

For the logoi and the angels are not really the same in a philosophical sense. While the powers are unbegotten, the angels are begotten.

---

[1] *Somn.* i. 19, abbreviated by Drummond.
[2] *Somn.* i. 21.

" Though the powers were not necessarily angels, the angels were most certainly powers [1]."

But the angelic appearances in the Old Testament served in the most acceptable way to furnish an allegorizing medium through which the philosophical Jew might convey both to his Gentile and Jewish readers his doctrine of the Divine powers, and their relation to men and the world.

The logos of Plato, which has sometimes been forced into an unnatural support of a doctrine of a Divine Trinity, became a foremost and favourite term with the Jew of Alexandria. But we must be careful not to exaggerate the signification of the term as used by Plato. If, not the master, but his disciples, used the phrase ξυναποτελῶν κόσμον, ὃν ἔταξε Λόγος ὁ πάντων θειότατος ὁρατόν, which occurs in the *Epinomis*, it cannot be made to appear that either Plato or his Jewish disciple really held a Trinity of Persons, though Plato's " obscurity allows room for an ingenious fancy to impose a meaning upon him [2]." The logos in the above passage is reason, which depends upon the true knowledge of number and proportion, and leads on to wisdom, harmony of soul, virtue, and happiness, so that "it does not immediately relate to the

---

[1] Drummond, vol. ii. ch. v. p. 147.
[2] Newman's *Arians*, I. iii.

creation of the world, nor does it at all express the personality of the logos[1]." The cosmos spoken of is the Pythagorean universe, displaying the regular and beautiful motions of order marked out by the Divine wisdom.

Yet there are foreshadowings of the Alexandrian logos in the writings of Plato. He recognizes an all-pervading reason in the universe. This he calls "Mind," νοῦς; but at the same time the terms of which Philo makes such use, "Logos," and "Wisdom," σοφία, are also employed in an exalted sense. The planets took their rise ἐκ λόγου καὶ διανοίας θεοῦ. He speaks of the "Divine reason and knowledge," λόγος τε καὶ ἐπιστήμη θεία. "In the conception of a cosmical soul, different from and yet mysteriously related to the supreme God, Plato does not indeed anticipate the Alexandrian philosophy, but he approaches some of its characteristic ideas more nearly than any previous thinker, and uses one or two of its characteristic expressions. . . . He extends to the Cosmos, or to its noblest part, the heaven, modes of expression which we might expect to find limited to the rational soul itself. If God begat the Logos, so also He was the 'Father' who 'begat this universe[2].' If the Logos was, according to the Johannine

---

[1] Caesar Morgan, *Trinity of Plato*, p. 5 (Camb. Ed. .
[2] *Tim.* 41 A.

proem, the only-begotten [1], so too, with Plato, was the heaven or the Cosmos [2]; nay, like the Logos, it was itself a 'god,' and an image [3] of the supreme [4]."

Plato's cosmogony in the *Timaeus* is a popular rather than a philosophical exposition, expressing his personal belief rather than the logical outcome of his system. There is given, first, the Deity, or Creator; secondly, the ideal world or archetype; and thirdly, the primitive matter. "But the later Platonists of the Alexandrian school adopted a different interpretation." They assumed the existence of an impersonal supreme principle. To this, "the ideal good, they assigned the highest place in the scale of existence, placing the intelligent author of the world, whom Plato calls the ever-existent God ($\ὢν\ ἀεὶ\ Θεός$), in the second rank ... and adding to these a third principle, the soul of the universe, the product of the Divine intelligence. These three constituted the celebrated Platonic, or rather Neo-Platonic, triad of $τἀγαθόν$, $νοῦς$, and $ψυχή$, which some of the Fathers regard as an approximation to the doctrine of the Holy Trinity, and which has been employed for two opposite purposes in modern times, by Cudworth in support of Christianity, and by Gibbon in depreciation

---

[1] Μονογενής.
[2] *Tim.* 31 B; 92 C.
[3] Εἰκών.
[4] Drummond, vol. i. ch. ii. p. 3.

of it. But in truth this triad, though attributed to their master by Plotinus and others of the Neo-Platonic School, cannot without extreme violence be extorted from the text of Plato himself, nor fairly traced, in its complete form, to any teaching earlier than the Christian era. . . . Nor can any greater weight be attached to another argument, also employed by some of the Fathers, in support of a Platonic anticipation of Christ, from the use by Plato and other philosophers of the term λόγος, to denote the Divine intelligence; a term which, whether intended literally or figuratively, will be naturally used in relation to the Divine mind, as it is in relation to the human, and which, in its earlier use, bears no trace of the theological signification afterwards assigned to it [1]."

But the doctrine of the Logos, regarded as an attempt to bridge the gulf between the eternal Being and the universe, though owing its terminology and its form to the influence of Greek philosophy, and even to various schools in it which did not recognize a transcendent Cause, came to its fuller expression in the mingled Graeco-Hebrew philosophizing of the Alexandrian Jew.

There was the term, with its concomitants, and Philo made great use of it. "By the Logos

[1] Article in Kitto's *Bibl. Encyclopaedia.*

Philo understands the power of God or the active Divine intelligence in general; he designates it as the idea which comprises all other ideas, the power which comprises all powers in itself, as the entirety of the supersensuous world or of the Divine powers[1]." He gives Nature the title, calling it the sacred Logos or reason, ἡ φύσις ... ὁ ἱερὸς λόγος. Here we discern the Stoical form of the conception. His meaning when using the terms λόγος θεῖος and λόγος θεοῦ seems to be really the Divine intellect. When we find him describing the κόσμος νοητός, or intelligible world, which is the reason of God, and the abstract form of the universe—the εἰκών and the σκιά of God—we are not surprised to read that "the shadow of God is His Logos, or reason, which He used as an instrument or organ when He made the world[2]." The intelligible world is called the elder, or firstborn Son of God; the sensible world His younger Son[3]. The "eternal entities, which reveal themselves as archetypal patterns through the visible objects of creation, form collectively, through their orderly combination, an intelligible cosmos[4], which is the archetype of the perceptible[5]."

---

[1] Schürer, *Jewish People*, Div. II, vol. iii. § 34.
[2] *Leg. All.* iii. 31.   [3] *De Conf. Ling.* 14. 1 ; 4. 14.
[4] Κόσμος νοητός.   [5] Drummond, vol. ii. ch. v. p. 79.

He advances to a sort of shadowy Trinity, which however is not by any means, nor could it be to him, as a Jew not forsaking his traditional faith, what the same idea is to us. The Deity is attended by two shadowy powers, or δυνάμεις. In the midst is the Father of all, "who in the sacred Scriptures is called by a proper name, Ὁ Ὤν, and those on each side are the oldest and nearest powers of the Self-existent, of which one is called Creative, and the other Regal. And the Creative is θεός, for by this he deposited and arranged everything into a cosmos; and the Regal is Κύριος, for it is right for that which has made to rule and hold sway over that which has been produced [1]."

On the words, "The Lord appeared to Abraham [2]," Philo explains that it was not the Self-existent Cause, but one of the powers around Him, that really appeared, namely, the Regal; because "Lord" is an appellation of sovereignty. What Philo means is, that God revealed Himself under different aspects, according to the receptive power of the soul to whom He appeared. Similarly in the visit of the three Angels. "God and His two principal powers are in reality one subject, though presenting to the understanding a threefold mental image."

Yet again, writing *De Cherubim*, which re-

[1] *Abraham* 24. 5. [2] Gen. xvii. 1.

present these two powers, the goodness and sovereignty of God, he introduces between them the Logos, expressed by the flaming sword. This connecting link, as it were, displays the truth that it is by His Logos that God governs and is good. The Logos represents the plan upon which the Divine action in creation and government proceeds[1]. Yet there is no Christian Trinity to be discerned in this. "There is no consistency in Philo's exposition, either as regards the number or the nature of these Divine powers. ... We find in one of the above passages the three beings all distinguished from the supreme God; while in another He seems to be identified with some of them. ... He has no more difficulty in finding six Divine powers to be represented by the six cities of refuge than he has in finding three to suit the two cherubim and the flaming sword[2]."

The general design of the universe Philo calls λόγος. The designs of the several parts are pluralized as λόγοι. These are the ministers and powers of the Divine Being, by whom or which also the intelligible world, archetype of the sensible, was formed.

To take Philo's λόγος to signify the Second

---

[1] See Trench, *N. T. Synonyms*, lxx.
[2] Mansel, Art. *Bibl. Encycl.* See Philo, *Prof.* 18, 19; also Qu. et Sol. in Ex. ii. 68, the Ark and five powers under the Supreme.

Person of the Divine Trinity in the New Testament sense, would be going far beyond his own thought. Yet there are passages in the Holy Scriptures resembling such as these. The "angel" in Acts vii. 38 would be with Philo a λόγος, as his λόγοι in turn are "by custom called ἄγγελοι."

Philo's system and bent of thought doubtless tended towards a personification of the λόγος. But he was a Jew, and therefore never really advanced to this conception. "Was the personified logos to be a second God, or was he to be nothing more than a created angel? If the latter, then he would lose all those lofty prerogatives and characteristics, which, Platonically speaking, as well as for the purposes of mediation and creation, were so entirely necessary to him. If the former, then Philo must break with the very first article of the Mosaic creed; he must renounce his Monotheism. Confronted with this difficulty, the Alexandrian wavers in piteous indecision; he really recoils before it. . . . After all that he has said, his logos is really resolved into a mere group of Divine ideas, into a purely impersonal quality included in the Divine Being [1]."

But if Philo had before him the Platonic doctrine of Ideas, he had behind him the belief

---

[1] Liddon, *Bampton Lectures*, ii.

in a Divine Kochmah or Wisdom in the Scriptures of his nation.

There is certainly a resemblance in that almost personified Wisdom to the Platonic Idea. Who has not admired the magnificent representation in the Book of Job? the co-eternal, part-creating, reigning joy of God in the Book of Proverbs? And in the non-canonical Sapiential books, the Son of Sirach[1] sings of Wisdom who is from all eternity with God, and is poured out on all His works[2]. She is to dwell in Jacob, and make her inheritance in Israel[3]. She resides in the Holy Law, which Moses commanded. Wisdom seems to be both a spiritual and yet physical power, perpetually manifesting herself to the sons of men. Nor is this Divine σοφία less glorious in the Book of Baruch. But in the Book of Wisdom she is ἡ ἀπαύγασμα φωτὸς ἀϊδίου[4]. Her sphere is not Israel and Palestine only, but the world and humanity.

And in the Targums there was the "Memra," or Word of God, which in the Sapiential books is the σοφία. In Ecclus. xliii. 26 the Logos is creator of the world; in Wisdom xviii. 15 a minister of judgement.

[1] Drummond, Bk. II. v, seems conclusively to show that this book was not influenced by Alexandria.
[2] Liddon, *Bampton Lectures*, ii; Ecclus. i. 1-10.
[3] Ecclus. xxiv. 8-12.
[4] Wisdom vii. 26; cp. Heb. i. 3. See p. 66.

Λόγος seems to be personified in the poetical sense so often applied to the Word of God in the Old Testament.

Here Philo, as we have seen, applies straight to Stoic and Platonic thought in order to draw out his system, with all its hesitations and uncertainties. The logos is with Philo (1) a Divine faculty: he uses λόγος as identical with νοῦς; (2) the Divine activity; (3) the ideal world, νοητὸς κόσμος, God's firstborn Son; (4) the Divine principle in the actual world, κόσμος αἰσθητός[1], which is God's younger Son.

But Philo means "Reason," not so much "Word" of God. The "Memra" of the Targums meant *Word* only; but when Philo found the term logos in the Greek Scriptures, he, eclectic genius that he was, gave it a meaning in which the Stoic, Platonic, and Hebraic senses were combined. The religious word was turned into the metaphysical, and his logos has no connexion either with the Messiah of Israel, or specially with the history of his own people. Sometimes with him it seems to take a personal meaning; sometimes an attributive; and once is actually termed a δεύτερος θεύς, though only, of course, ἐν καταχρήσει[2]. In *Fragments* ii. 625[3], Philo

---

[1] Dorner, *Pers. of Christ*, Introd. and Notes I, J.
[2] Euseb. *Praep. Evang.* vii. 13.
[3] Answering to Qu. et Sol. in Gen. ii. 62.

asks, "Why, as though speaking of another God, does He say, 'I made man in the image of God,' but not in His own image?" And he answers, that nothing mortal could be made like the Father supreme, but only like the "second God," the logos (τὸν δεύτερον θεόν). Because in the soul of man the rational impress must be stamped by the Divine Reason, and cannot answer to *God* as its archetype, who is above Reason.

Plato divided the world into νοητά and αἰσθητά. Philo, in a corresponding manner, makes a Stoical division of the logos—ἐνδιάθετος and προφορικός. Yet, while acknowledging a distinction in the logos of the universe, he never actually uses the above terms except as applying to the logos in man. In a leading passage he says [1], "The logos is twofold both in the universe and in the nature of man. In the universe there are both that which relates to the immaterial and pattern ideas, . . . and that which relates to the visible objects. . . . But in man the one is inward and the other uttered; the one as it were a fountain, but the other sonorous."

It may be that Philo was "distinctly and fully aware of a failure in the analogy between Divine and human speech. So long as the Word was regarded as simply an expression of thought it might, without irreverence, be attributed to the

[1] *De Vit. Mos.* iii. 13.

Divine Being; but as soon as it was defined by an epithet which was proper only to spoken and audible language, it ceased to be applicable[1]."

The appearance in Philo of this distinction, though only partial, as well as his general use of the term Logos, seems to make it clear that he wrote under the joint influence of the Greek philosophy and the language of the LXX. "In the use of the cognate term σοφία, as nearly if not quite equivalent to that of λόγος, he was probably more directly influenced by writers of his own nation, by the LXX version of the Proverbs, and by the Books of Ecclesiasticus and Wisdom[2]."

In the account of the λόγος μεσίτης the thoughts of the Greek philosophy, the conceptions of the Hebrew Scriptures, and a foreshadowing of the ideas of Christian theology, are curiously blended together. Philo says, "The Father who generated the universe gave a special gift, that standing on the borders it should separate the created from the Creator. . . . And it exults in the gift, and with dignity tells of it, saying, 'And I stood between the Lord and you[3],' being neither unbegotten as God nor begotten as you, but in the middle between the extremes, serving as a pledge to both; on the side of Him who planted, for a security that the race

---

[1] Drummond, Bk. III. ch. vi. p. 180. [2] Mansel.
[3] On Deut. v. 2.

will never wholly depart and vanish, through choosing disorder instead of order; and on the side of that which has grown, for a ground of hope that the propitious God will never overlook His own work [1]."

It has been pointed out, that we have here the Pythagorean στοίχια, the Aristotelian doctrine of a Mean, and the μεσίτης or Mediator of the New Testament, as it were thrown together in confusion.

Less frequently Philo makes use of the term "Spirit" (πνεῦμα). He gives it two senses. "The Spirit of God," he says, "signifies in one sense the air, the third element; and it is used in this sense at the beginning of Genesis, where it is said, 'the Spirit of God was borne above the water.' . . . In the other sense, it is the pure wisdom in which every wise man participates [2]." On Exod. xxxi. 2, 3, he comments, "God called up Beseleël and filled him with Divine Spirit, wisdom, understanding, knowledge," "so that what Divine Spirit is, is defined through these terms." This Divine Spirit can remain, but not permanently, in the soul, because hindered and oppressed by the flesh. As it is said, "My Spirit shall not continue to remain in men for ever, because they are flesh."

Philo identifies the Spirit, then, with Wisdom, and that in a transcendent sense, generically,

---

[1] *Quis rer. div. haer.* 42 (i. 501-2).   [2] *Gigant.* 5.

and therefore makes it ontologically the same as the Logos.

The Stoics, in a physical sense, spoke of God as "Spirit." And the ready transmutation of such terms as λόγος, σοφία, πνεῦμα, into persons, as well as the gradual personification by the Greeks of νοῦς, λόγος, πνεῦμα, helps us to see how abstract terms began to stand out with an identity of their own; so that with Philo, familiar with this use, the term λόγος came apparently, if not really, to signify the vision of God granted to men in the writings of Moses.

Thus, while observing that Philo never really anticipated the glorious doctrine of a personal Mediator in the eternal Son of God, we see that the language he adopted, in his attempt to utilize his acquaintance with philosophy in interpreting or allegorizing his own Jewish Scriptures, and to reconcile the "wisdom" of the world with the revelation of his own people, led on to a new phraseology and thought-atmosphere which could not be without its effect and utilization, either in the Gnostic dreams that were to have their day, or in the presentation of Truth which was to break over the darkness of men's minds. The "gnosis," falsely so called [1], would be, and partly by help of the same weapons, met and counteracted in the Evangel of the Christ.

---

[1] Ψευδώνυμος γνῶσις. 1 Tim. vi. 20.

IV.

THE LOGOS IN THE NEW TESTAMENT.

WHILE it is difficult, as we have said, to declare in many instances with certainty whether the similarities which meet us in the New Testament to the thoughts and phrases of heathen philosophy are really derived from that source, or are only parallels, resulting from accident or from a common atmosphere of thought, this difficulty is greatly increased by the uncertainty of the dates of some of the New Testament writings, as, e.g., St. Paul's Epistles as compared with Seneca; St. John as compared with the development of Platonic ideas and Gnostic thought, &c. Were we able to place certain of the New Testament writings, as some would do, a good way down into the second century, much might be asserted that otherwise can only be surmised. But this would be at the cost of much that is precious in regard of the genuineness of some of these New Testament passages, and as conflicting, in our view, with a truer chronology. We may therefore be unable, while observing parallels, to assert that they are necessarily *traces* of the Greek philosophy in the New Testament. And where the traces may be more safely asserted, it is to be remembered that while in the Christian use these words and ideas become greatly enhanced and even changed in their definiteness and profound value, there is really more than a mere use made of this material of philosophy. Much may be owing to thoughts and ideas latent in the human mind as such, and therefore common to both. But beyond this, as Dorner points out, in reply to those who seek to disparage Christianity on account of these existing parallels, the peculiarity of Christianity, " in a theoretical respect, (is) in this, that in it, as the organism of the truth, the elements of truth, elsewhere here and there to be met with in a scattered form or a disfigured guise, come together in unity—a unity which, as it personally appeared in the God-man, so in the course of history ever more and more rises upon the consciousness of mankind." And again: " whilst the ground-idea of Christianity cannot be elucidated either from heathenism or Judaism, in and by itself, there yet lies in it that which both, from very different sides, seek and forebode [1]."

(1) That around which our deepest interest gathers in the New Testament, as connecting it, through Alexandria, with the Greek philosophy, and that which also is of the greatest import as regards the Christian theology, is the doctrine of the Logos, which finds its highest development and its conscious expression as a philosophical term in St. John. But before proceeding to consider it, a brief digression may be allowed in order to glance at some terms used by St. Paul, which may be regarded as in a manner breaking up the ground.

As λόγος with St. John, so νόμος with St. Paul

[1] *Person of Christ*, Introd.

On the other hand, with regard to Philo himself, if we look beyond the New Testament days, with which only we are now concerned, to the subsequent development of philosophical ideas within the Church, we shall see that, instead of looking upon him as a fountain-head of Christian doctrine, it may be more correct to regard him as the unconscious source of heresy. "To say nothing of Philo's influence upon the theosophizing Fathers of the Church, Clement of Alexandria and Origen, who borrowed largely from their Jewish predecessor and fellow-citizen, some of the salient heresies of the early centuries had almost their spring in the Philonian writings; . . . while the Pagan philosophy, the Neo-Platonism of Alexandria, which derived much of its strength and obtained its ultimate defeat from the Christianity which it both aped and hated, is mainly traceable to our Philo." Note to Dr. Holmes' article on "Philo" in Kitto's *Bibl. Encyclopaedia*.

is an oft-repeated and characteristic word, and helps us in the present inquiry. St. Paul does not confine its use to the Law of Moses; with him it is a much wider term, and sometimes almost personal. The word in its ambiguity and wider sense was common to the Greek and the Jewish world. In this way it was also itself a "trace" of the Greek philosophy. With Philo there was not a wide distinction between the λόγος and the idea expressed in νόμος. If the world was created by the λόγος, by the λόγος it was bound together, as by an all-embracing law: ἀπὸ τῶν μέσων ἐπὶ τὰ πέρατα συνάγων τὰ μέρη πάντα καὶ σφίγγων [1]. In the *De Immut. Dei*, 30, he speaks of the Divine Word as "ever running about the world to establish the perfect form of government —universal democracy." If St. Paul speaks of the law of God as "holy [2]," and "spiritual [3]," and "good [4]," and declares that he "rejoices in it after the inward man [5]," and St. James pronounces a blessing on the man who "looketh into the perfect law of liberty," we find Philo using almost similar language: ὅσοι μετὰ νόμου ζῶσιν ἐλεύθεροι. Νόμος δὲ ἀψευδὴς ὁ ὀρθὸς λόγος, οὐχ ὑπὸ τοῦ δεῖνος ἢ τοῦ δεῖνος θνητοῦ φθαρτὸς ἐν χαρτιδίοις ἢ στήλαις ἄψυχος ἀψύχοις, ἀλλ᾽ ὑπ᾽ ἀθανάτου φύσεως ἄφθαρτος ἐν ἀθανάτῳ διανοίᾳ τυπωθείς [6].

[2] i. 562.   [2] Rom. vii. 12.   [3] vii. 14.   [4] vii. 16.
[5] vii. 22.   [6] ii. 452.

And St. Paul's language concerning a law written on the heart[1], even where no positive or pen-written law had been given, seems much like an echo of this; though, as we shall by-and-by see, it is more than likely that he drew also from his knowledge of Roman law for much of this kind of terminology and illustration, especially in writing to Romans; and it is not unreasonable to suppose that at one and the same time there was a combination of ideas from both Greek and Roman sources in the mind of the great apostle, as he wrote with the eloquence of rapid and comprehensive thought.

In Rom. v. 20 St. Paul says, "the law entered that sin might abound." In vii. 9 he says that "when the commandment came sin revived." This has been pointed out as paralleled in Philo by his explanation of Lev. xiv. 36, where the priest, entering the leprous house, has to pronounce on its uncleanness. Philo makes the priest the λόγος, and spiritualizes the passage so as to apply it to the soul. Here we have, says Jowett, "a dimmer expression of St. Paul's often repeated thought, 'Sin is not imputed where there is no law,'" &c.; and we see at this stage the two ideas of the λόγος and the νόμος very much as one.

Moreover, Philo speaks of the λόγος ἔλεγχος entering the human soul (ii. 195), as, in the type

[1] Rom. ii. 14, 15.

of Balaam, it rebukes the erring will. It is also the παράκλητος in ii. 247.

With St. Paul, the powerful agent in the conviction of sin is the νόμος of God. But the brief glance we have just taken suffices to show how the ideas expressed and combined under these terms were serving the purpose of linking thought.

In Gal. v. 14 St. Paul uses both νόμος and λόγος in a similar sense, though with a differing degree of meaning, making the νόμος the written law, and the λόγος the brief and complete expression of it.

(2) In opening the First Epistle to the Corinthians we meet with language which, as it applies directly to the sophistical teaching and showy rhetoric of the day, has its use also in bringing out the better σοφία and higher γνῶσις of the Gospel[1].

In i. 17 ff. the apostle is giving a description of his preaching among the Corinthians, who were lovers of philosophical speculation, disputation, and rhetoric. As he was not sent for the special purpose of administering the ritual of the faith ("not to baptize"), so neither was he sent to put forth an intellectual system, a σοφία. The Corinthians had, some of them, turned from St. Paul in greater admiration of

---

[1] See also to the Ephesians and Colossians.

Apollos, who, as an eloquent Alexandrian, would be acceptable to them on account of his style of address, more like that to which they were themselves addicted than the plain unadorned speech of the apostle himself. Οὐκ ἐν σοφίᾳ λόγου refers plainly to the substance and matter[1], not to the mere form of his message. He deprecated the speculations of philosophy, "lest the cross of Christ should be deprived of its effect;" and this would result less by rhetorical eloquence than by the "wisdom of words" of the "disputer." Οἱ ἀπολλύμενοι are the lovers of this earthly σοφία, for it is to them that the preaching of the cross is mere μωρία. Nevertheless, these "σοφοί," of which the Greeks had ever thought so much, are themselves a perishing race, for God shall destroy them. "Where is the philosopher?" he asks. (Where is the Rabbi?) "Where is the reasoner, the sophist, of this passing age? God hath turned the very σοφία of this world into μωρία? For since the world, in the wisdom of God Himself, failed by means of its own wisdom to gain a knowledge of God (which was the manifest result of the now dead age of philosophy), it pleased God by the (so accounted) μωρία of preaching to save them that believe. It is true that the Jew leans his faith on a sign, and that the Greek demands a philosophy; but

---

[1] *Second Stoical Sense*, D. i. p. 111.

the Christian messenger simply proclaims a fact, that of a crucified Messiah; and in this fact there is what both seek; for the Jew a mighty work, a power which is indeed a sign; for the Greek a philosophy which will not be superseded by the fancies of the next school; for both the sign and the wisdom are of God Himself." And proceeding in the eloquent contrast, he sums it up in the magnificent statement that "Christ is to us, from God, a σοφία par excellence, a wisdom which is at once a practical power to cure all the ills of humanity, being righteousness, and sanctification, and redemption."

And further, the apostle shortly urges (ii. 6 ff.) that this wisdom which is from God is a wisdom which can only be truly known by the initiated; for it is in μυστηρίῳ, revealed only to the μύσται. Yea, it is πνευματικοῖς πνευματικά. This is the Christian and the true doctrine of "similia similibus percipiuntur." Strange and ridiculous as some forms of that old theory were among their philosophers, it is here absolutely true. The πνεῦμα of God can alone reveal to the πνεῦμα of man the things that are God's alone.

And therefore the old philosophers were right when they said (Plato, *Phædo*, &c.) that the man who lived an earthly and sensual[1] life dragged down his soul until it was impossible

---

[1] Wisdom i. 2-4, &c.

for it to be really free and to soar above. So now, the ψυχικὸς man (the word is more definite under the light of Divine truth) is unable to perceive or to receive what to the πνευματικὸς man is made clear by the πνεῦμα of God. Platonism [1] had called the Divine Spirit, or inspiration, πνεῦμα; and so indeed it is. It cannot touch the merely ψυχικὸς man [2].

All this shows the inevitable contact which took place between St. Paul's message and the terms and professions of philosophy which existed in his day.

Πνευματικός was, moreover, the epithet specially claimed by the party of Apollos. But the *real* πνευματικός, says St. Paul, is the man taught by the Spirit of God. On the other hand stands the ψυχικός, the man endowed with the "anima," the living principle of the world, the ἐντελέχεια σώματος of Aristotle [3], the οὐσία καὶ ἐνέργεια σώματός τινος [4].

St. Paul, as a pupil of Gamaliel, who combined in his teaching both Alexandrian and Jewish views, in respect of the use of the terms before glanced at, spoke mainly according to the Jewish school. Hence we do not find him using the

[1] Ax. 370 C.
[2] Philo's "good" and "bad" men are distinguished as σαρκική (ψυχή) and λογική.
[3] See below, p. 82, on St. Paul's teaching.
[4] *Metaph.* 7. 3, 1; *de Anima*, 2. 1, 5, &c. See Plat. *Tim.* 30 B. sqq.

word λόγος as personally applied to the Son of God. In this school, Origen declares[1] that he could not find any holding τό, τὸν λόγον εἶναι τὸν υἱὸν τοῦ Θεοῦ. Nevertheless, we find σοφία, πνεῦμα, νόμος, frequently in St. Paul;—we find him speaking of the νόμος of God almost as Philo speaks of the λόγος;—we find that Philo identifies the λόγος with the σοφία of God. In St. Paul, Christ is the σοφία. In St. John, He is the λόγος. Thus the way is prepared for a fuller use of these and kindred terms in Christian theology.

(3) Doctrinally between St. Paul and St. John stands the Epistle to the Hebrews[2]. If not written by Apollos, it was at least the work of some disciple to whom the Alexandrian gnosis was by no means unfamiliar. It is impossible to read the opening sentences without seeing this. With special reference to the point before us, chap. i. 3, and chap. xi. 3, speak of all things being upheld τῷ ῥήματι τῆς δυνάμεως αὐτοῦ, and of the ages being framed ῥήματι Θεοῦ. The term λόγος is not used; but the thought is there. We might venture to say that ῥῆμα here is the λόγος προφορικός of Philo. It is the utterance of the power of God, the "breath of His mouth." But in iv. 12 we have the term λόγος, evidently

---

[1] *Cont. Cels.* ii. 31.
[2] The Epistle itself is separately considered below, p. 65.

under the same conception, which is actually, as with Philo, the *dividing word*, τομώτερος ὑπὲρ πᾶσαν μάχαιραν; as in Philo[1], the τομεὺς λόγος[2].

But in all this the Word is not personal. The context in the passages referred to shows that if the Son of God had been meant the term would have been again applied, which it is not. Nevertheless, we are drawing near to the λόγος of St. John. If the Gospel of St. John was written at Ephesus, it was written where the Alexandrian gnosis had made a home.

(4) St. John takes a splendid leap of thought. He wrote much later. Philosophical terms were widely current, and Alexandrian thought was widely spread. A dangerous gnosis, a false theosophy, was threatening the peace of the Church and the purity of the Truth. The apostle, inspired and filled with the spirit of the Christ, whom he had known face to face, seized the term which was so full both in history and meaning, and made it the property of the faith for ever. All that was true in the old philosophical thought, in the λόγος of Plato, in the ἰδέα ἰδεῶν, εἶδος εἰδῶν; all that was true in the "Memra" of the Jews, and in the Angel of God's Presence; all that was true in the σοφία

---

[1] *Quis div. rer. haer.* i. 491, &c.
[2] See Alford's full note in loc., and Jowett, *St. Paul and Philo.*

of the Sapiential books, in the λόγος of Philo himself, in the θεῖος λόγος, in the δεύτερος θεός, in the πρωτόγονος, in the εἰκὼν θεοῦ, in the γενικώτατος, in the ἄνθρωπος θεοῦ, in the ὁ κατ' εἰκόνα ἄνθρωπος, in the λόγος μεσίτης, in the λόγος ἐνδιάθετος and the λόγος προφορικός [1]—all this and much more the apostle boldly claimed for the Son of Man, the Christ of Israel, the eternal Son of God, the Life and Light of all creation.

There was no personality in the logos of the old philosophy; there was no thought of Incarnation in the logos of Philo. St. John outstrips every thought that had feebly striven for birth, and at once embraces them all in his magnificent statement, Ἐν ἀρχῇ ἦν ὁ λόγος, καὶ ὁ λόγος ἦν πρὸς τὸν Θεόν, καὶ Θεὸς ἦν ὁ λόγος. . . . Καὶ ὁ λόγος σὰρξ ἐγένετο, καὶ ἐσκήνωσεν ἐν ἡμῖν. The exordium of the Gospel, as of the First Epistle, lays the foundation upon which all that follows is to be apprehended. This done, the apostle proceeds with historical fact, with Divine teaching. Enough that "the Word, from the bosom of the Father, was made flesh, and dwelt among us," "the Light and the Life of men;" that this Life we "have seen, and handled, and declare unto you." "The Logos," says Jowett, "in the Alexandrian sense, occurs in the New Testament only at the commencement of the Gospel of St.

[1] St. John i. 18.

John" (for in the Epistle, earlier in date, it takes rather its Christian sense and spiritual glory)—" it has a single definite application to the person of Christ. It is like an expression borrowed from another system, the language of which was widely spread, and for once transferred to Him; no further doctrinal use is made of the term." But then he proceeds with his wondrous story. This λόγος was Christ Jesus, the Prophet of Nazareth, the Incarnate Son of God.

In the Greek philosophy, God was not to be apprehended by man. He was ever more and more distant. Of the Eleatic "One" nothing could be predicated. The Platonic ἰδέαι raised a barrier between the Being and Phenomena. In Philo, the tendency was the same. Philo's δυνάμεις, introduced as mediators, only put the eternal Being at a greater distance, and the λόγος fades into an impersonal idea. In St. John, God and man meet face to face, and we see "Emmanuel, God with us."

For the Logos was eternal, the Logos was essentially Divine. In the statement of St. John, the Logos was already in existence when all things began; He was "with God," and therefore personal; He was Himself God. The whole universe was His workmanship, and therefore He was no mere agent or intermediary by which the Infinite could deal with the finite.

"No man hath seen God at any time [1];" but yet "the only-begotten Son, which is in the bosom of the Father, He hath declared Him." The Word is not, as regards the eternal One, πρωτόγονος, but μονογενής. In fact, the Logos on earth is to men indeed "very God."

The chasm that separates the old philosophers, as well as Philo, from the teachers of the New Testament, consists in the fact that whereas with the former, the infinity of the supreme Being, and His transcendence above the world, necessitated the invention of some intermediate link between the eternal and the phenomenal, a link needed even to enable God to create (an act which they considered impossible to Him, as directly performed), the latter showed in their inspired message that there is no such gulf fixed between the Supreme and His world; and offered to our view what neither Greek nor Alexandrian ever dreamed of—Deity Incarnate. The dogmatic faith of Judaism bridged the gulf without explaining it; the word of the Lord came to men; He sent His angels; how, they did not try to solve. The philosophy of Greece only made the chasm more hopeless; the Infinite *could not* communicate with the finite. But while Plato and the Stoics, as well as Philo, introduced Form, Reason, δυνάμεις, the Logos, logoi, and so on, as

---

[1] See below, p. 69.

intermediary agents, the New Testament sounds forth the profound mystery, Θεὸς ἦν ὁ λόγος [1]. And in the practical, personal application of the profoundest doctrines to the Christian life, St. Paul allows of no metaphysical intervention between the human soul and God. "All are yours; and ye are Christ's; and Christ is God's" (1 Cor. iii. 23). "I would have you know, that the head of every man is Christ; and the head of the woman is the man; and the head of Christ is God" (1 Cor. xi. 3).

(5) It remains that we glance at the remarkable title given in the Apocalypse (xix. 13) to the King of kings, as He goes forth at the head of the armies of Heaven. "His name is called ὁ λόγος τοῦ Θεοῦ."

The Son of God is spoken of in the same book as "the first and the last," "the beginning of the creation of God"; and immediately following the application of the term λόγος is a description of His power in the words of Old Testament prophecy.

---

[1] "The ideal Logos, the distinguishing feature of the Alexandrian philosophy, has no place in the teaching of the New Testament. The belief in one Christ, very God and very man, has not only no place in, but is diametrically opposed to, the philosophical speculation of Philo."—Mansel.
This remains true, while we still admit the special appreciation of the term by St. John, in the words of Jowett as quoted above (p. 60).

If we assume the quite late date of the Apocalypse, placing it last of St. John's writings, the term as here used seems to come in in a natural way, the τοῦ Θεοῦ being consistent with the historic setting of the picture, as τῆς ζωῆς is in agreement with the spiritual teaching of the First Epistle.

But if, though late, we take it to be earlier than the Gospel, the true explanation seems to be, with Bishop Westcott, that "in these phrases we find the earliest form of the 'Logos doctrine,' which is still kept within the lines of the Old Testament ideas. But the later unfolding of the truth is included in this earliest confession [1]."

So that, this being the earliest indication, and the ὁ λόγος τῆς ζωῆς of the First Epistle a fuller development of the thought, the λόγος of the Gospel gives us the final and complete teaching, which fell like a seed into the soil of the Church, to bear fruit in future ages.

---

[1] Westcott, *St. John's Gospel*, Introd.

V.

KINDRED TRACES.

VARIOUS ELEMENTS IN THE EPISTLES OF THE NEW TESTAMENT.

As a book, the Epistle to the Hebrews stands more directly between Alexandria and the rest of the New Testament than any other writing, and in style and form is thus a link between the latter and the old philosophy. At the risk of repetition here and there, we take it next in order. Though, as regards the rest, as parallels and traces are not found upon any system, we shall not be able to confine ourselves in order to any one book or Epistle.

The Epistle to the Hebrews is essentially Alexandrian, both in its Jewish and Greek elements. Its allegorical treatment of the Old Testament, its uniform use of the LXX version, its Alexandrian language, are alike striking.

Its opening lines, stately and philosophical, are a fitting introduction to the whole systematic work.

God has in old time spoken by the prophets to the fathers in divers portions and manners. But now, to us, by a Son.

The communication is therefore direct and superhuman. Who is this Son?

First, the heir of all things, and framer of the ages (ch. i. 3).

This is He who presently becomes the pre-existent Logos of St. John. He is the ἀπαύγασμα of the δόξα of God. Ἀπαύγασμα is a Philonean term (i. 337 ; ii. 356), and is found in the Book of Wisdom, vii. 26, ἀπαύγασμα φωτὸς ἀϊδίου. This is more than "reflection." It is the emanation, radiance, effulgence, of the Divine glory [1].

This, afterwards the φῶς ἐκ φωτός of the Creed, "seems to have been universally the sense among the ancients.... The Son of God is, in this His essential majesty, the expression, and the sole expression, of the Divine Light— not, as in His Incarnation, its reflection." Philo, de Concup. ii. 356, has, on Gen. ii. 7, τὸ δὲ ἐμφυσώμενον δῆλον ὡς αἰθέριον ἦν πνεῦμα καὶ εἰ δή τι αἰθερίον πνεύματος κρεῖττον, ἅτε τῆς μακαρίας καὶ τρισμακαρίας φύσεως ἀπαύγασμα—that is, a ray of the Divine Nature itself. How important this term afterwards became in the controversies of the Church is well known.

[1] See p. 43.

Χαρακτὴρ τῆς ὑποστάσεως αὐτοῦ is specially interesting here.

Philo, *Quod. det potiori ins.* § 23 (vol. i. p. 217), designates the πνεῦμα imparted by God to man τύπον τινὰ καὶ χαρακτῆρα θείας δυνάμεως; Moses naming the same εἰκών, to show ὅτι ἀρχέτυπον μὲν φύσεως λογικῆς ὁ Θεός ἐστι, μίμημα δὲ καὶ ἀπεικόνισμα ἄνθρωπος: *de plant. Noe*, § 5 (p. 332), he says, "Moses named the rational soul τοῦ θείου καὶ ἀοράτου εἰκόνα, δόκιμον εἶναι νομίσας οὐσιωθεῖσαν καὶ τυπωθεῖσαν σφραγῖδι Θεοῦ, ἧς ὁ χαρακτήρ ἐστιν ὁ ἀΐδιος λόγος. Here the λόγος is designated as the impress of the seal of God, by the impression of which in like manner on the human soul, this last receives a corresponding figure, as the image of the unseen and Divine" (Bleek).

τῆς ὑποστάσεως αὐτοῦ. The later controversies concerning this word and the term οὐσία do not come in here. The word bears the meaning of essential being, substance. From signifying "sediment," "support," "foundation," the word had come to mean actual existence, and then the *real underlying nature*, thus equalling οὐσία; of which use the passage before us is probably the earliest example (Liddell and Scott).

All this, though not reflecting in a special sense philosophical thought, is essentially philosophical in spirit, and forms a very interesting link between the old axiomatic system of

Hebraism and the speculative, inferential conclusions of the Grecian method. In the Epistle to the Hebrews revealed religion claims philosophy as her handmaid.

"Upholding all things by the Word of His power."

We have seen that the thought of the Logos lies dormant in the phrase; but it is the *Son* who upholds; and this is connected with the previous statement. The Son is the effulgence of God's glory and the express image of His essence. But He is verily also the Creator. "Philo had described the Word as an effulgence, and spoken also of Him as distinct from God. But in Philo these two statements are inconsistent. For the former means that the Word is an attribute of God, and the latter means that He is a creature. The writer of the Epistle to the Hebrews says that the Word is not an attribute, but a perfect representation of God's essence. He says also that He is not a creature, but the Sustainer of all things. These statements are consistent [1]."

As St. John (i. 3), so also St. Paul in Col. i. 16, 17, makes the same grand statement of the Son, who is thus implicitly the Logos in the Christian sense. He is "the εἰκὼν τοῦ Θεοῦ τοῦ ἀοράτου, πρωτότοκος πάσης κτίσεως. For by Him were

[1] T. C. Edwards, D.D.

all things created, . . . visible and invisible, whether thrones or dominions, &c.; . . . He is before all things, and in Him all things consist."

Akin to this is the magnificent passage in 1 Tim. vi. 15, "Who is the blessed and only Potentate, the King of kings, and Lord of lords; who only hath immortality [1], dwelling in light unapproachable; whom no man hath seen, nor can see: to whom be honour and power eternal [2]."

This, of course, is inspired teaching, and essentially Christian; but yet the language and the thoughts carry us back beyond Philo to the conception of the transcendence of God in later Greek philosophy, "even outside the Platonic schools." The Greek had long conceived of God as the Absolute Unity. He was Absolute Being. Only the One really exists. Over against this are the Many, the objects of sense. "But the conception, even in this second form, was more consistent with Pantheism than with Theism. It was lifted to the higher plane on which it has ever since rested by the Platonic distinction between the world of sense and the world of thought. God belonged to the latter, not to the former. . . . In this sense God is transcendent ($\epsilon\pi\epsilon\kappa\epsilon\iota\nu\alpha$ $\tau\hat{\eta}s$

---

[1] Plato's word, *Phaedr.* 246, &c., ἀθανασία.
[2] Cp. St. John i. 18.

οὐσίας), beyond the world of sense and matter. 'God therefore is Mind, a form separate from all matter; that is to say, out of contact with it, and not involved with anything that is capable of being acted on[1].'" In a note Hatch adds, "This is a post-Platonic summary of Plato's conception; into the inner development, and consequently varying expressions of it in Plato's own writings, it is not necessary to enter here. It is more important in relation to the history of later Greek thought to know what he was supposed to mean than what he meant. The above is taken from the summary of Aetius in Plut. *de Plac. Philos.* 1, 7 ; Euseb. *Praep. Evang.* 14, 10. The briefest and most expressive statement of the transcendence of God (τὸ ἀγαθόν) in Plato's own writings is probably *Repub.* p. 519, οὐκ οὐσίας ὄντος τοῦ ἀγαθοῦ, ἀλλ' ἔτι ἐπέκεινα τῆς οὐσίας πρεσβείᾳ καὶ δυνάμει ὑπερέχοντος."

He then quotes Plutarch: "What, then, is that which really exists? It is the Eternal, the Uncreated, the Undying, to whom time brings no change.... God is: and that not in time but in eternity ... and being One, He fills eternity with one Now, and so really 'is,' not 'has been' or 'will be,' without beginning and without ceasing[2]."

And Maximus of Tyre: "It is of this Father

[1] *Hibbert Lectures*, ix.   [2] *De Ei ap. Delph.* 18.

and Begetter of the universe that Plato tells us: His name he does not tell us, for he knew it not: nor does he tell us of His colour, for he saw Him not; nor His size, for he touched Him not.... The Deity Himself is unseen by the sight, unspoken by the voice, untouched by fleshly touch, unheard by the hearing; seen only—through its likeness to Him, and heard only—through its kinship with Him, by the noblest, and purest, and clearest-sighted, and swiftest, and oldest element of the soul [1]."

And Philo, who did not need to go to the Greek thinkers to conceive of God as One and Eternal, is a link in the process of expression. "The words, 'I am thy God,' are used not in a proper but in a secondary sense. For Being, *qua* Being, is out of relation [2]; ... He transcends all quality [3] ... He is not in space ... He is not in time [4] ... He is 'without body, parts, or passions [5]'; ... He is invisible, for how can eyes that are too weak to gaze upon the sun be strong enough to gaze upon its Maker [6]? He is incomprehensible [7]: ... we know *that* He is, we cannot know *what* He is: we may see the manifestations of Him in His works, but it were monstrous folly to go

---

[1] 17. 9.   [2] *De Mut. Nom.*, 4; i. 582, ed. Mangey.
[3] *De Mund. Opif.* 2; i. 2.
[4] *De post. Cain*, 5; i. 228, 229.
[5] *Quod Deus immut.* 12; i. 281.
[6] *De Abrah.* 16; ii. 12.   [7] i. 224, 281, 566, &c.

behind His works and inquire into His essence[1]. He is hence unnamed[2]."

(2.) Kindred with these thoughts are those suggested by the language of Heb. xi. 1–3. Here we have the great definition of faith, faith in general, which leaps the barriers of sense, passing by phenomena, and sees, knows, the things which are out of sight.

It has been said that without the gift of imagination faith would be impossible. So far as this is true, we must place the imaginative genius of Plato, his aspiring visions of the Good and the True, in the same category with this triumphant faith of the soul that sees beyond phenomena. Philo's notion of faith was that of this passage, and Plato's soaring visions were akin to the same, though we admit the difference in degree.

"Faith is the hypostasis of things hoped for." Is the word exactly the same in sense as in i. 3? Quite the same it obviously cannot be; but it is as strong in the mental idea introduced. Faith brings the very *ousia* before the soul as if it had it in possession. It is the *substantiating* of the things not perceptible by sense.

---

[1] *De post. Cain*, 48; i. 258.
[2] Compare with this language the words of St. Paul in Rom. i. 20: "For the invisible things of Him from the creation of the world are clearly seen ... even His everlasting power and divinity."

It is again the scrutinizing test, the realizing proof, ἔλεγχος, of that which puts mere phenomena into the ranks of the unreal.

Verse 3: "By faith we perceive that the ages have been framed by the word of God, so that what is seen hath not been made out of things which do appear."

Not from phenomena. Then surely from the ideas in the Divine Mind. Is there not a trace of Platonism here? Possibly. The language is appropriate. Not only is a personal Creator here asserted, but a Creator acting through the ideas and patterns of His own Mind. The thoughts revert to the language of viii. 5, where the writer, after declaring the Law to have served as a copy and shadow (σκιά) of heavenly things, adds the command of God given to Moses, "See that thou make all things according to the pattern showed to thee in the mount."

A little lower down, xi. 10, the language is not only philosophical, but suggests a double philosophical idea: "He looked for the city which hath the foundations, whose τεχνίτης and δημιουργός is God."

Here, first of all, we have the thought of the pattern city, the ideal πόλις. "The Greek πόλις, the state, whose equivalent in modern times is not civil but ecclesiastical, was an ideal society, the embodied type of a perfect constitution or organization.... The Stoical definition of a πόλις was σύστημα καὶ πλῆθος ἀνθρώπων ὑπὸ νόμου διοικούμενον[1]. Its parts were all interdependent and relative to the whole; the whole was flawless and supreme, working out without friction the Divine conception which was expressed in its laws. The world was such an ideal society. (The idea is found in almost all Stoical writers.) It consisted of gods and men: the former were its rulers, the latter its citizens. The moral law was a reason inherent in human nature, prescribing what men should do, and forbidding what they should not do: human laws were but appendages of it. In this sense man was a citizen of the world [2]."

And the Ideal State of Plato, as well as the later "City of God" of St. Augustine, were but forecasts and shadows respectively—with all such conceptions of the "Holy City," the "Heavenly Jerusalem"—of the Revelation of St. John, and of the city which is the "real" one with the foundations, pictured here by the writer to the Hebrews as the one to which Abraham looked forward.

But there is the τεχνίτης and δημιουργός, the very terms, not only of the Book of Wisdom and of Philo, but of Socrates[3] and Plato[4], δημιουργὸν

---

[1] Clem. Alex. *Strom.* 4. 26.
[2] Epict. *Diss.* 3. 22, 5; Hatch, *Hibbert Lectures*, viii. 1, and notes.   [3] Xen. *Mem.* i. 4, 7.   [4] *Tim.* § 9.

τοῦ κόσμου, &c., the meaning here being appropriately, "fabricator," not "creator."

(3) The writer of the Epistle to the Hebrews guards against the rising Gnostic error of the doctrine of emanations in his description of the glory of the Son as above all created angels. The Platonic Ideas, and Logos, with the Hebrew conception of the great I AM, thrown further into the background of the universe by Philo's Platonism and his vague notions of the Logos and the ἄγγελοι; these thoughts mingling with the Christian teaching of the person and work of the Mediator, though utterly out of harmony with it, made the new error dangerous and difficult to combat. The existence of a spiritual hierarchy, and of ministering angels, the writer fully admits [1], as do the other apostolic writers; but the Son is not of these; our Mediator is by no means an emanation, human or Divine; He is Himself both God and Man [2].

(4) As we proceed, Christ is seen to be the ἀρχιερεύς, even as the Logos of Philo. A nominal resemblance only, perhaps; for Philo never identified the Logos with the Messiah, which our Epistle does in the conception of thought. The Logos was over the universe of God. Christ is the Son over His own House.

---

[1] See also ch. xii.   [2] Ch. i, ii.

(5) "Philo had already emphasized the distinction between the child in knowledge and the man of full age and mature judgement. St. Paul (1 Cor. iii. 1-3, &c.) and St. Peter (1 Peter iii. 2) had said more than once that such a distinction holds among Christians. Many are carnal; some are spiritual. . . . In the Epistle to the Hebrews [1] the distinction resembles the old doctrine of habit taught by Aristotle. Our organs of sense are trained by use to distinguish forms and colours. In like manner, there are inner organs of the spirit ($αἰσθητήρια$), which distinguish good from evil, not by mathematical demonstration, but by long-continued exercise ($γεγυμνασμένα$) in hating evil and loving holiness [2]."

Aristotle was emphatic on the power of habit as a factor of first importance in the formation of character. Moral excellence is more dependent on habit than even on instruction or nature. He takes this law for granted, and as needing no argument [3]. He shows how in the artist's studio the work and the workman are distinct: "in the formation of character the workman is himself the work [4]." Even allow-

---

[1] Ch. vi.
[2] In order to keep to the Epistle, we here unavoidably anticipate an *ethical* trace.
[3] Grant, *Ethics*, i. 240. [3] *Ib.* ii. iv.

ing (as Christ in Matt. xxv. 15) that some have a better start in the endowments of nature than others, he insists on the responsibility attaching to habit, and will not allow it as an excuse for vice. As he assumes Free-will, so he insists on its exercise even here [1]. Virtue does not consist in gifts of nature, but only in cultivation by the principle of habit [2].

This line of thought, so different in its atmosphere from the allegorism of Philo and the Old Testament, and from the philosophical flights of Plato, is nevertheless brought in here by the writer with a very earnest purpose; and the downright urging to practical progress, the almost terrible force of this sixth chapter to the Hebrews, places the reader in the bracing air of the old ethics of the most earnest of philosophers, showing that whatever use the messenger of Christ may incidentally make of all surrounding helps, his purpose is not at all to add to the fancies of thought, or to speak "as man's wisdom teacheth," but, with the eye fixed on the tremendous reality that the eternal Son of God hath in these last days brought to light, to make men in earnest as he is himself, to show life, under the new light of the Sun of Righteousness, as something to be practically

---

[1] Grant, *Ethics*, iii. v. 17-21. [2] *Ib.* ii. v.

planned for and lived, with all the intensity that ever Stoic put into his philosophy, or Epicurean into the present moment [1].

(6) Platonism has been detected, and not without some reasonableness and beauty of thought, in verses 13–16 of this chapter.

"For they that say such things make it manifest that they are seeking after a country of their own." "Let not the full force of the words escape us. The apostle does not mean that they seek to emigrate to a new country. He has just said that they confess themselves to be ξένοι καὶ παρεπίδημοι. They are 'pilgrims,' because they are journeying through on their way to another country; they are 'strangers,' because they have come hither from another land. His meaning is that they long to return home [2]." He guards against being thought to mean Ur of the Chaldees. It was not the earthly home, which they had left for ever. "Yet they yearned for their fatherland (πατρίδα)."

The thought is that of Plato's reminiscences—the previous state of existence in which we saw something of the True and the Beautiful. We

---

[1] Cp. Philo's philosophical διδαχή, φύσις, ἄσκησις; and especially his νηπίοις ἐστὶ γάλα τροφή, τελείοις δὲ τὰ ἐκ πυρῶν πέμματα (i. 302) with the N. T. ethics, and with the almost identical language of Heb. v. 12, 13.

[2] T. C. Edwards, D.D.

have referred to this above, p. 26. And Wordsworth's lines recur,

"Our birth is but a sleep and a forgetting."

"Our author too suggests it; and it is true. We need not maintain it as an external fact in the history of the soul, according to the old doctrine, resuscitated in our own times, of Traducianism. The apostle represents it rather as a feeling. There is a Christian consciousness of heaven, as if the soul had been there and longed to return[1]." Of "God, Who is our home."

The question naturally arises, Does the inquiry put to our Lord in John ix. 2 reflect the old metempsychosis of Pythagoras, filtering through Plato and the Book of Wisdom, and associating itself with the Jewish conviction that all evil was the punishment of sin in some way? In the *Phaedo*, Socrates discusses with Cebes the question of the condition of souls who have lived sordid or animal lives on earth. He says to him:

"But if the soul depart full of uncleanness and impurity, as having been all along mingled with the body, always employed in its service, always possessed by the love of it, and charmed by its pleasures and lusts; ... Do you think, I say, that a soul in this condition can depart pure and simple from the body?

[1] T. C. Edwards, D.D.

"No, Socrates, that is impossible.

"On the contrary, it departs stained with corporeal pollution. . . . The soul loaded with such a weight, is dragged into that visible place, not only by its own weight, but by its own dread of the light and the invisible place, and, as we commonly say, wanders in cemeteries, among the tombs."

See St. Matt. viii. 28; St. Mark v. 2; St. Luke viii. 26, ff. The belief in demoniacal possession resembles this doctrine.

But Socrates continues:

"I say, Cebes, for instance, that those who made their belly their God[1], those enter into the bodies of asses, or such-like creatures. . . . The case of all the rest is much the same."

This is the doctrine from its darker side, the side of degeneration and moral failure, which was recognized by the philosophers of Greece, though they tried various ways of escaping from it. Plato would have God only the author of good, and referred evil to other causes. The Stoic denied the reality of apparent evils.

In the Book of Wisdom, viii. 20, the striking words occur, $\mu\hat{a}\lambda\lambda o\nu$ $\delta\grave{\epsilon}$ $\dot{a}\gamma a\theta\grave{o}s$ $\mathring{\omega}\nu$ $\mathring{\eta}\lambda\theta o\nu$ $\epsilon\mathring{\iota}s$ $\sigma\hat{\omega}\mu a$ $\dot{a}\mu\acute{\iota}a\nu\tau o\nu$; and in the passage in St. John we have the disciples of Christ asking the

---

[1] Note the term in Phil. iii. 19, where the "end," moreover, is destruction.

question about pre-existent sin as if the doctrine was quite familiar to them.

(7) In ch. viii. 6, ix. 15, xii. 24 of the Epistle to the Hebrews, we have the Christian doctrine of the μεσίτης or Mediator. The λόγος μεσίτης of Philo has been referred to above [1] as showing a curious mingling of Pythagorean, Aristotelian, and New Testament ideas.

(8) Finally, on this portion of Scripture, "Philo may be allowed to stand in a nearer relation to the Gospel of St. John, and to the Epistle to the Hebrews, than to any of the writings of St. Paul. There is a truth in saying that St. John wrote to supply a better gnosis, and that in the Epistle to the Hebrews a higher use is made of the Alexandrian ideas and the figures of the Mosaic dispensation. That is to say, the form of both is an expression of the same tendency which we trace in the Eastern or Alexandrian gnosis. But admitting this similarity of form, the difference of spirit which separates St. John or the author of the Hebrews from Philo is hardly less wide than that which divides him from St. Paul. The Logos of Philo is an idea, of St. John a fact; of the one intellectual, of the other spiritual; the one taking up his abode in the soul of the mystic, while the other is the indwelling light of all mankind [2]."

[1] Page 47. [2] Jowett.

Still further are the thoughts of inspiration removed from the Ideas of Plato, and the conceptions of the terms of Greek philosophy. But the streams by which the various waters have mingled, through nation and nation, age and age, bringing together the Chosen People,—worshippers of the One Self-revealing God, the Mystics of the East, the Thinkers of the West, and the apostolic messengers of the newly known and final Logos of God, the true Λόγος σπερματικός [1], which, coming ever into the world, was the Light through the ages to every man who was a seeker after God—these streams may be traced with ever-widening interest, showing us that never at any time God left Himself without witness.

(9) Before leaving this division of our subject, reference must be made to the remarkable teaching of St. Paul on the threefold nature of man. It is true that Holy Scripture generally speaks of man's soul and body, or of his spirit and his flesh, or of the opposition of the spirit against the flesh, as if man were simply a dualistic being. But underlying this there is a very distinct trichotomy which cannot be held to contradict it. Further back we mentioned the contrast insisted on by the apostle between the spiritual and the natural

---

[1] Compare St. John i. 4.

man, the πνευματικός and the ψυχικός[1]. In Rom. viii. 10 we find the apostle contrasting the *body* and spirit, speaking of the σῶμα as dead, while the πνεῦμα lives. In a preceding verse (5), he contrasts the *flesh* and spirit, σὰρξ καὶ πνεῦμα; and numerous passages might be similarly quoted. But out of them all we gather, that while ψυχή and σῶμα may be spoken of in contrast, as in St. Matt. x. 28, and on the other hand, as in St. Paul, ψυχή and πνεῦμα, the ψυχή may at one time be spoken of as the vehicle of the πνεῦμα, and at another as the life-principle of the σῶμα[2]. But in 1 Thess. v. 23 there is a summing up of the complete man: ὁλόκληρον ὑμῶν τὸ πνεῦμα καὶ ἡ ψυχὴ καὶ τὸ σῶμα ἀμέμπτως τηρηθείη. This striking analysis helps to make clear those passages where the contrast is from the one side or the other considered as dualistic. Here we have πνεῦμα for the immortal and divinely communing part of man; ψυχή for the lower or animal soul, in which are the passions and the desires, and which, while it may on the one hand be drawn up and ennobled by the πνεῦμα, as in the πνευματικοί, may on the other be simply reigning as the agent of the σῶμα or σάρξ, as in the σαρκικοί or the ψυχικοί. St. Jude has the ex-

---

[1] Page 57.
[2] See Delitzsch, *Bibl. Psychol.* iv. sect. iv. passim.

pression, ψυχικοί, πνεῦμα μὴ ἔχοντες; because in such the πνεῦμα is crushed down under the lower ψυχικός nature, now become σαρκικός.

It is impossible for the mind not to recur to the anthropology of Plato. He speaks of ψυχή, the animal soul, as αἰτία κινήσεως ζωικῆς ζώων[1]; and his trichotomy, as well as that of Aristotle, is in form, not terms, like St. Paul's. "For the soul of passion and the soul of desire (θυμική and ἐπιθυμητική) are, according to Plato, mortal; and to the latter he adjudges sensibility (αἴσθησις); so that it occurs at least as a consequence of his system, that to this mortal twofold portion of the soul are to be generally appropriated the forms of activity common to man with the brute. And Aristotle, who in like manner declares that the sustaining and sensitive soul (θρεπτική and αἰσθητική) is decaying, and only the reason (νοῦς, and indeed the νοῦς ποιητικός) is immortal, attributes to this immortal soul expressly not merely appetite (ὄρεξις), but, moreover, sensuous perception, imagination (φαντασία), memory (μνήμη), recollection (ἀνάμνησις), and thus every activity of the soul that belongs to the brute also[2]."

And Plato constructs his model state on the outlines of the tripartite man. The working classes answer to the appetitive element, and must be under the control of the military order,

[1] *Def.* p. 411.   [2] Delitzsch, *Bibl. Psychol.* ii. sect. iv.

answering to the emotive or passionate θυμός; and this must develop itself in dependence upon the reason, by gymnastic training and music, and from it the governing classes will proceed, answering to the rational soul in the man [1].

In 1 Cor. xv. 44, 46, St. Paul contrasts the σῶμα ψυχικόν with the σῶμα πνευματικόν which is to be. On other occasions, as will be seen, where ψυχικός takes a moral sense, it is depreciatory. This, says Trench in his extremely interesting remarks on these terms in *New Testament Synonyms*, is characteristic of the inner differences between Christian and heathen, and indicative of those better gifts and graces which the dispensation of the Spirit has brought into the world. Ψυχικός, continually used as the highest in later Greek classical literature—the word appears first in Aristotle—being there opposed to σαρκικός [2], or, where there is no *ethical* antithesis, to σωματικός [3], and constantly employed in praise, must come down from its high estate, another so much greater than it being installed in the highest place of all. That old philosophy knew of nothing higher than the soul of man; but Revelation knows of the Spirit of God, and of Him

---

[1] Plato, *de Repub.* ii. 368; viii. 544, &c. See below, p. 94.
[2] Plut. *Ne Suav. Vivi Posse*, 14.
[3] Aristotle, *Eth. Nic.* iii. 10. 2; Plut. *de Plac.* i. 9; Polyb. vi. 5. 7.

making His habitation with men, and calling out an answering spirit in them [1].

In Holy Scripture, God is πνεῦμα; and τὸ πνεῦμα is the Holy Spirit, by which the Deity holds communion with the πνεῦμα of man. It would be deeply interesting, were this the place, to pursue the consideration of the development of the Nous, Logos, Pneuma, as representing the Trinity in the Divine Nature after which man is formed. "Humanity is θεοῦ γένος precisely for that reason, that it is essentially distinguished by means of the λόγος from the ἄλογα ζῷα, which know that which they know—φυσικῶς, not λογικῶς [2].... That in man which wills, thinks, and experiences, is called in general πνεῦμα, as God is the tri-personal πνεῦμα. But in this self-conscious πνεῦμα are distinguished νοῦς, λόγος, and πνεῦμα— a representation of the Father, Son, and Spirit [3]."

Here also we may draw attention to the striking passage in St. Paul's First Epistle to the Corinthians [4], concerning the first and second Adam. After asserting the spiritual (πνευματικόν) body as complementary to the natural (ψυχικόν) body, he says, "The first man, Adam, became a living soul (ψυχὴν ζῶσαν); the last Adam, a life-giving spirit (πνεῦμα ζωοποιοῦν)." As throwing

[1] § lxxi.
[2] Jude 10.
[3] Delitzsch, *Bibl. Psychol.* iv. sect. v. See above, p. 57.
[4] xv. 45, 47.

some light upon this thought we have Philo's idea of the twofold creation: first, the heavenly (οὐράνιος), that is, the ideal man; then the earthly (γήϊνος) man[1]. "But then, such illustration is rather an example of how Philo is corrected by St. Paul, than of how St. Paul borrowed from Philo[2]." This is perfectly true; and we do well to remember that the New Testament, in taking up the thoughts which had dawned with partial light in philosophy, illuminates them by the fuller light of revelation. We are assured of the grand truth, that God hath never left Himself without witness.

(10) And the history of all such terms, as of εἰκών, ὁμοίωσις, ὁμοίωμα—κόσμος, αἰών—σοφία, φρόνησις, γνῶσις, &c., would show the student how not the New Testament only, but all subsequent Christian theology, is indebted to the old Greek philosophy for the means of expressing thoughts and conceptions which, going far beyond what the thinkers of those days had in mind, would have been without adequate expression at all but for the work already done by those "seekers after God."

(11) Of this the great doctrinal passage in Phil. ii. 6, 8 is a striking example. The eternal

[1] *De Alleg. Legis.* i. 12, 13; and *De Mundi Opif.* 46. Observe also St. Paul's terms, χοϊκός, ἐπουράνιος, in vv. 47-49.
[2] P. Holmes, D.D., in Kitto's *Encycl. Bibl.*, art. "Philo."

Son of God, ἐν μορφῇ Θεοῦ ὑπάρχων, was of the very essence of God. He nevertheless became most truly man, μορφὴν δούλου λαβών. The Incarnation was a veritable fact. In outward presentation He was found σχήματι ὡς ἄνθρωπος, and therefore men despised and rejected Him [1].

Here is no utterance of philosophy. And yet the revelation of so tremendous a fact would have failed of expression but for the terms which philosophy had furnished and made adaptive.

(12) In 2 Peter iii. 5-10 there is a very striking passage, consisting of a glowing prophetical description of the end of the present order of the visible world. As the flood of water in Noah's days destroyed the then world, so at the end of this age οἱ οὐρανοὶ ῥοιζηδὸν παρελεύσονται, στοιχεῖα δὲ καυσούμενα λυθήσονται, καὶ γῆ καὶ τὰ ἐν αὐτῇ ἔργα κατακαήσεται.

Can it be that here we have, in Stoical dress perhaps, a presentation of the ancient theory of Heraclitus, according to which the destiny of the universe was, as under the law of eternal flux, alternate phases of creation and conflagration? We would not venture to say that the theory is accepted in its bareness; but the likeness is there, even though inspiration should

---

[1] See Lightfoot's interesting discussion on μορφή and σχῆμα in his *Epistle to the Philippians*. Also Trench, *N. T. Synonyms*, on μορφή, σχῆμα, ἰδέα, § lxx.

have made the outlines of the event more sharp, definite, and solitary. If we do not assume the genuineness or authenticity of the Epistle, the difficulty as to the special point is less. There was the first creation. There will be the conflagration. Then there will be a re-creation of the heavens and the earth. But this is in agreement with the prophetic passages also in the Revelation of St. John.

(13) In the Epistle to the Ephesians, and its companion one to the Colossians, St. Paul dwells on the great idea of the Christian State, and its realization in the Church. There are sublime depths of wondrous beauty; depth under depth lie beneath the surface for repeated study and discovery. The first Epistle especially is the statement of a divinely grand philosophy, not handed down from the schools, not taught by men. Christ is the centre of it; the Head over all things to the Church; the Firstborn of all creation. In Him all things are summed up and gathered together, and in Him God is glorified to the ages of the ages.

Again, here is no heathen philosophy. But may we not say, that one office of the philosophy of Greece was to make it possible for such an Epistle to be written? That men's minds should have received the training necessary to enable them to apprehend and receive the immensity of such revelations, was no slight matter. And surely here we see once more a result, a service ordained of God, by which all that was in the world, besides that which was specially imparted to the Chosen People, was in the hand of the Eternal as His servant to the truth.

The apostle here lays open before his readers the mysteries of a Sophia, a Phronesis on the part of God, which for man should be a **gnosis** surpassing all the wisdom of the past and all the theosophy of the present. Nor in the future should a rival to it ever appear; for it was the " knowledge-passing love of Christ," the **Pleroma** of God, which should be to them and to all men eternally satisfying.

ETHICAL PHILOSOPHY.

VI.

PLATO, ARISTOTLE, STOICISM, THE EPICUREANS.
(THE FOUR SCHOOLS.)

WE shall not expect to find anything like direct traces of Aristotle in the New Testament. This great philosopher, this great moralist, distinguished by his exceeding earnestness, directness, and honesty, was long neglected after the time of his first two successors. Before the time of Cicero, but slender traces of a knowledge of his writings are discoverable. The popular taste was not for his severer works, but for a rhetorical treatment of his *Ethics*. Even the school itself declined, as in devotion to the master, so in splendour and influence. His writings were too abstruse and difficult for a superficial generation to unfold. As he himself had said, his writings "had been published and yet not published." He was known through extracts and anthologies, while he himself was relegated into the shade. But a revival took place when with the library of Apellicon, carried off from Greece by Sulla, the works of Aristotle were unearthed to new and eager eyes. Tyrannion and Andronicus of Rhodes did much by the pains they bestowed on the precious relics.

But even then, it was less as a philosopher than as a moralist that he became really known. Cicero took up, as a Roman might be expected to do, the *Ethics* and the *Natural History* rather than the sterner and more abstruse parts of his philosophy.

As an ethical teacher, therefore, we may reasonably suppose that Aristotle's influence made itself felt through eclecticism, the works of Cicero, perhaps through the Stoics and Seneca, whose store of gathered material was immense.

It will at least be interesting to glance very briefly at some points in Aristotle as compared with Plato. Certain terms we meet with in the New Testament, with their trains of thought, bear kinship with both[1].

Aristotle's reasoning is chiefly inductive. Starting from what he knows, from the bare fact, he rises to the potentiality of the principle embodied and exemplified. Imagination is not allowed the play with him that it is given in

---

[1] See above, on Heb. vi, p. 76, &c. Some ethical parallels have been unavoidably anticipated.

Plato. This is at once seen in their different notions of the Ideas. With Socrates they were mere abstractions; with Plato absolute existences; with Aristotle they are void of all existence apart from the things in which they find realization.

(1) One important feature is common to both Plato and Aristotle: the union of Ethics with Politics, so that one is a necessary part of the other. Each has his State, his city, with which the individual is bound up. But while Plato's State is an ideal one to which nothing on earth can correspond, that of Aristotle is the goal to which each man must make it his duty to conform his life.

The highest purpose of action is happiness. This is the ἐνέργεια of life existing for its own sake, the perfect life, according to virtue also existing for its own sake, perfect virtue. While the happiness of the life of reason, the diviner life, is accorded to but few, that of the active, practical life, based in ethical virtue, is more or less open to all. But this can only take place in the *State*; and thus Ethics lead on to the doctrine of Politics. Happiness depends upon virtue (ἀρετή) followed out in accordance with this idea. Family life is the model, resembling monarchy[1], and "in it lie the germs

[1] *Pol.* I, 7.

of friendship, constitution, and all that is just[1]."

With Plato, on the other hand, Virtue, and therefore Happiness, is only attained in the soul's perfect harmony, beauty, and health. Its tripartite faculties must work in mutual peace and agreement. As all that is real is found in the Divine Ideas, so true Virtue is assimilation to God. As his psychology, like St. Paul's, is threefold, so is his State, for it is a copy of the true individual life. The workers, the military order, the governing body, must work in harmony like the appetitive element, the emotive element, and the rational faculty, in man[2].

This glance will show that certain passages in St. Paul are of special interest as touching our subject, even though we may not venture to assert that the apostle was directly acquainted with the writings of these great philosophers.

(2) STOICISM, originally springing from an eastern seed, but travelling westward, and growing and systematizing on a Grecian soil, had been again transplanted for cultivation in a Latin home. Here its speculative elements gave way to a stronger growth as an ethical system, and supplied a moral vocabulary which was no less valuable as an aid to Christianity

---

[1] *Eth. Eudem.* vii. 10. [2] See above, pp. 83 ff.

than the sister development of theological terms through the medium of Alexandria.

But it was, says Lightfoot, "like all the later systems of Greek philosophy, the offspring of despair. Of despair in religion: for the old mythologies had ceased to command the belief or influence the conduct of men. Of despair in politics: for the Macedonian conquest had broken the independence of the Hellenic states, and stamped out the last sparks of corporate life. Of despair even in philosophy itself: for the older thinkers, though they devoted their lives to forging a golden chain which should link earth to heaven, appeared now to have spent their strength in weaving ropes of sand. The sublime intuitions of Plato had been found too vague and unsubstantial, and the subtle analyses of Aristotle too hard and cold, to satisfy the natural craving of man for some guidance which should teach him how to live and to die [1]."

The language of Stoicism became widely diffused, and the Stoic philosophy itself had a central home at Tarsus, the birth-place of the Apostle of the Gentiles. It is therefore by no means surprising that there should be discovered in the writings of St. Paul, at least, a familiarity with dogmas and maxims which belong to this school, and which, in the transforming light of

---

[1] Lightfoot, "St. Paul and Seneca," in *Ep. to the Philippians*.

the revelation of the Son of God, were capable of becoming watchwords full of life and strength, and expressive of a spirit which belonged to Christianity alone; even as, on the other hand, there are undoubted reflections of the light of Christianity in later Stoicism itself. The truth indeed being, that the modified Stoicism of Seneca, and the terms which, borrowed from the older philosophies, were familiar to his pen, represented the philosophical element of the day in which the thoughts of men floated.

Stoicism professed a rule of life, which gave it some strength and originality, though the phrase of "living in conformity with Nature" needs a little explanation to save it from misrepresentation.

A first cause and a governing mind, said that school, are evidenced by the order of universal nature. He is Reason. He is the Creator. And yet their creed was really Pantheistic. God is after all the eternal substance, varying in its form and moods; the primary matter and the efficient force which shapes it. From this God all things proceed, and to Him they will at last return. This God is a fiery ether, as in the philosophy of Heraclitus, and in the end the material world will dissolve in fervent heat, and the Divine substance alone remain [1].

[1] Comp. 2 Pet. iii. 10-13. See p. 23.

Thus material things alone were real. And the Stoical forms of speech were fatalistic. Yet it was not impossible for a Stoic to address, as in the hymn of Cleanthes (see Acts xvii. 23), almost a devotional lyrical prayer to the First Cause. Indeed, much of the language of the disciples of the school far transcends the ultra-materialism of their professed belief. The dignity of God and man; the moral order of the world; the special privilege of the human being, so nearly allied to the Eternal Reason; the possibility of the soul's existence after death, and of its undergoing a purgatorial discipline, or of perishing as the result of evil and foolish living on earth, redeems the system from being a mere useless speculation. To follow what is really best, most fit, considering the design and end of nature; this is the moral code, and it demands a life well ordered in conformity with a law of conduct. There is a pleasure of calmness and serenity following such a life; but it is not pursued as an end, virtue being essentially its own reward.

At the same time the ἀπάθεια which characterized the system, forbade emotion, or passion of any kind, even pity and sympathy, beyond what may issue in usefulness. See that the intentions are good; cultivate the individual soul in its proper sphere, and regard death as a good end, to be even courted in some circumstances.

But this severity and coldness became much tempered in time, and Seneca, the contemporary of St. Paul, wrote much that was so admirable and so like to the maxims of Christianity, that the attempt to prove a mutual knowledge and correspondence between the apostle and the philosopher need not occasion great surprise. But by that time Stoicism was itself eclectic, and even the sayings of Epicurus were borrowed where agreeable in sentiment, as e.g. "initium est salutis notitia peccati[1]."

But such terms as "peccatum" will not bear the full Christian sense; and the Christian Church of Jerome's time erred in supposing that the "Sacer Spiritus," "salus," "caro," which might be spoken of as transfigured ("transfigurari"), "sacramentum," "caritas," were synonymous with the Christian terms, though the parallel was striking.

Yet after the older philosophies, after Platonism, represented in Alexandrianism, and distorted in the Oriental admixture of the Gnostics, Stoicism it is which seems to find most parallels of expression in the writings of the New Testament, although those parallels may not be really connected. For the maxims

[1] *Ep. Mor.* 28. 9.

and sentiments of the school were widely spread, and the morality they presented met the cravings of a practical age when philosophy as such was little needed.

(3) Of Epicureanism there is little to be said. Possessing no literature to speak of, it was more a fashion of life than anything else. It has been termed atheistic, which is practically true of it, yet it was not the pleasure-theory of the Cyrenaic school from which it sprang. Epicurus himself was remembered and revered as a man of pleasant manners and prudent life. His "society" set a wholesome example, and the calmness of life which resulted from the removal of the fear of the gods and of death was the preparatory soil in which their doctrines of quiet happiness were reared. We shall not find it touch the New Testament in any important way, though a brief reference or two is to be found. It announced that "virtue alone is inseparable from pleasure[1]," and that to live wisely, nobly, and justly, means to live happily[2]. It is evident that with the multitude this teaching would soon degenerate into the lowest sense of "Let us eat and drink, for to-morrow we die," though if that motto was not really representative of Epicurus' doctrine, St. Paul may have had such men in view in 1 Cor. xv. 32. The

[1] Diog. Laert. x. 138.   [2] Ib. 140.

words which immediately follow, "Evil company doth corrupt good manners," are a line from the *Thais* of Menander.

The Epicurean was his own providence. Whatever the chances of life might be, it was in the power of a reasonable man to work out his own happiness. No over-mastering destiny drags us along; the gods have let us alone. Τὸ παρ' ἡμᾶς ἀδέσποτον [1].

It is not impossible that St. James had in view the danger and atheism of such ideas when he warned his readers (ch. v. 13 ff.) against planning for the morrow with overweening and selfish confidence. He is addressing those outside the Church, or at least those who readily fall into the worldly spirit so opposed to Christianity, of which he has already spoken so severely. Among the Jews of the Dispersion the floating Epicureanism of the day might be a real snare.

The words of our Lord in Matt. vi. 34 have the air of an adage. If a popular saying, is there any reason to suppose they might not be an echo of the Epicurean proverb, "He who is least in need of the morrow will meet the morrow most pleasantly [2]"?

But we proceed to some more striking ethical parallels and traces.

---

[1] Diog. Laert. x. 133.   [2] Plut. *De Tranq. An.* 16.

VII.

Ethical Traces.

(1) St. Paul, in a remarkable sentence in Eph. iii. 15, derives "every family in heaven and earth" from one model and archetype, the Divine Πατήρ of the universe, and of the Church, which is on earth especially His πατρία, embodying the true idea, which is a fundamental one, of the family constitution and relationship. A very large and important part of Christian ethics arises from this root conception of the family of God, one on earth and in heaven, with its relations of every kind in word, deed, and conduct, spreading outwards, and affecting mutually all the members.

In the same Epistle (iv. 16) the Head, which is Christ, is that from which the whole body of the Church, the spiritual State, is fitly framed and knit together, and so is increased and built up in love. In ch. v. 23 he instances the relation of husband and wife as again a copy of the archetypal union between Christ and His Church; and in the words which follow he insists upon the real and actual oneness that is between the Divine Head and all the members of the living body.

In writing to the Colossians he brings forward the same image in i. 18 and in ii. 19; the words being almost identical, as the idea is the same.

There is no proof, of course, that the apostle, in speaking of these high and holy "mysteries," had in mind at all the thoughts and imagery of the old philosophers; but if he possessed knowledge, direct or indirect, of the principles of philosophy as taught by its great thinkers, his language in these passages would be very natural.

If we may venture to think that the Alexandrian Epistle to the Hebrews, in ch. xii. 22, 23, is not only contrasting Sinai and Zion, but in the glowing language used is also picturing the ideal city, the perfect State, as Plato pictured it; may we not suppose that the conception given us by St. Paul of the heavenly State founded on the family is a reflection of the State of Aristotle, which is also founded on the family? The arrangement of the domestic system in *Polit.* i. 7 is monarchical, while at the same time the family images political life generally. The germs of constitution, friendship, and justice, lie in the family¹.

The purpose of the State Aristotle considers as the unity of a whole consisting of mutually dependent and connected members.

(2) But there is more in it than lies here. The word Conscience, Συνείδησις, is very frequent in St. Paul. The Christian is a man of conscience. And the Christian conscience has become a very tender and exacting monitor. It is to him the voice of God Himself, seeing that it rests its authority on His holy Law².

It is true that the term συνείδησις³ is not found in Aristotle; "there is not indeed the unhesitating and unequivocal enunciation of self-knowledge, self-acquittal, self-condemnation, which is the inheritance of the Christian ethics. ... He makes the reason the Judge, presiding over this court ever in session within the man, rather than the advocate, laying his case before the will, whose verdict is final. Conscience, with Aristotle, is not the voice of God⁴." The man himself, the general voice of the best of mankind, the enactments of the State, &c., are the sanction upon which conscience, with Aristotle, must depend. But the point here is this. Aris-

---

¹ *Eth. Eudem.* vii. 10.   ² Rom. ii. 15.
³ See below, p. 118, on Stoicism.
⁴ Gregory Smith; see *Ethics*, IX. iv. 5, 10.

totle, like Plato, merges his ethics in politics; and even denies the higher exercise of virtue except as in the State. So also his idea of conscience is intimately bound up with the same thought. With him man is essentially a political being. He exercises his noblest energies as part of a social organism. The community overshadows the individual [1].

Still, as the notion of a family and a state organism are found as essential parts of Aristotle's *Politics*, so a real idea of conscience is developed in his *Ethics*. And as the ideal man represents the community, so the ideal man is the judge of moral rectitude. He is σπουδαῖος [2], or the man in earnest. He is φρόνιμος [3] and πεπαιδευμένος [4], fully equipped, κεχορηγημένος [5]. The term φρόνησις is perhaps the nearest approach to the idea of conscience in the Christian sense. It pronounces specifically what is good [6] and enjoins duty to that end [7].

This prepares us to see in Rom. ii. 14, 15 something of the spirit of these pronouncements. The heathen, even φύσει, τὰ τοῦ νόμου ποίει. He is supplied by the light of reason and conscience. Aristotle, in his *Ethics*, V. x. opposes the φυσικόν

---

[1] See *Ethics*, I. vii. 6.   [2] *Ib.* III. iv. 4.
[3] *Ib.* II. vi. 15.   [4] *Ib.* I. iii. 4.
[5] *Ib.* I. x. 15.   [6] *Ib.* VI. v. 5.
[7] *Ib.* VI. x. 2.

to the νομικόν. There are moral dictates enjoined by the Law. But these men 'Εαυτοῖς εἰσι νόμος ¹, reason and conscience having supplied the place of this Law. So Aristotle² says the enlightened man will so conduct himself as being law to himself—οὕτως ἕξει οἷον νόμος ὢν ἑαυτῷ.

(3) Conscience is implied also in Aristotle's delineation of the struggle between right and wrong in the man who, not having fallen away altogether from good, is yet not among those who are above the pain of conflict. He asserts "something in our nature different from reason, contrary to and contending with it³." This contradictory element in us is not insensible to the voice of reason, and may be corrected unless allowed to gain the upper hand⁴. Control of the passions, therefore, is necessary, and thus Aristotle brings in his immortal doctrine of ἐγκράτεια.

Are we not at once carried to St. Paul's great chapter on the struggle in the inner man, in the seventh chapter to the Romans? Is there anything essentially different in the description itself? The apostle views the matter, of course, from the vantage-ground of the victorious believer in Christ, as a man who can now count himself among the πνευματικοί. And in Gal. v.

---

¹ Rom. ii. 14. ² *Ethics*, IV. xi.
³ *Ib.* I. xiii. 15; III. xii. 7; VII. iii. 11.
⁴ *Ib.* I. xiii. 15.

23 he names ἐγκράτεια among the special fruits of the Spirit; as before Felix he reasoned later on of ἐγκράτεια, as well as of righteousness and judgement to come [1].

(4) While Aristotle looked upon self-regard as the motive to virtue, he yet gave a twofold meaning to justice. On the one hand, it included in the domain of duty every obligation to others; on the other, in a narrower sense, it was the observation of contracts and engagements. In *Ethics*, V. i. 15, he makes justice specially the virtue that has reference to the advantage of others, τελεία ἀρετὴ πρὸς ἕτερον, and then he adds (*ibid.* 18) that this constitutes its special difficulty. While thus his morality is selfish, it yet resembles that which is of mere maxim in Christianity; and, divested of the warmer, higher altruism which abounds in the context, the pithy sentences of Rom. xiii. 7–10, have an echo of the same; ἀπόδοτε πᾶσι τὰς ὀφειλάς· τῷ τὸν φόρον τὸν φόρον, τῷ τὸ τέλος τὸ τέλος, τῷ τὸν φόβον, &c., and at the end, ἡ ἀγάπη τῷ πλησίον κακὸν οὐκ ἐργάζεται· πλήρωμα οὖν νόμου ἡ ἀγάπη.

(5) In Phil. iv. 5 St. Paul urges upon Christians the duty of moderation, or reasonable forbearance, in which consideration, and not strictness of right, would rule their conduct as regards others. This ἐπιεικές is like that which,

---
[1] Acts xxiv. 25.

with Aristotle, "fills up the necessary deficiencies of law, which is general, by dealing with particular cases as the law-giver would have dealt with them if he had been by." *Eth. Nic.* V. x. 6 διό, δίκαιον μέν ἐστι, καὶ βέλτιόν τινος δικαίου ... καὶ ἔστιν αὕτη ἡ φύσις ἡ τοῦ ἐπιεικοῦς, ἐπανόρθωμα νόμου, ᾗ ἐλλείπει διὰ τὸ καθόλου. And (*ibid.* 8) the ἐπιεικής is ὁ μὴ ἀκριβοδίκαιος ἐπὶ τὸ χεῖρον.

Aristotle insisted, that where friendship is at hand to guide, justice with her strict demands is not needed. So also Christianity teaches, that "he that loveth another hath fulfilled the law." Only that Christian love is a higher grace; its action is much wider and more unselfish.

(6) With regard to the true worth of moral actions, Aristotle taught that the intention, which alone stamps the action as good or evil, is implicit and only partly operative until crowned by opportunity. Thus the προαίρεσις waits for contact with actual realities before its true character is displayed. We are reminded of St. James (i. 15), "When lust hath conceived, it bringeth forth sin," &c. And much of the Sermon on the Mount, which is sometimes compared in a disparaging sense with the old philosophic morality, might be cited in the same way.

But we are not at liberty to suppose that mere likeness points to contact or relationship.

The old philosophy was feeling after goodness as well as knowledge, and inevitably approached the Truth again and again; and when the Truth itself came in reality and with authority, much of its speech must perforce resemble some of what had gone before. While one was a prevision of the other, the other was not necessarily a reflection of the one. Rather, both were founded on the eternal rock of eternal verity, and man, lightened more or less in all ages by the Light of the world, caught glimpses of the Radiance that was ever the same, and bore witness to one Law and one Conscience [1].

While, therefore, we have selected some of those passages in the New Testament which seem to point to a knowledge or an indirect reflection of the moral philosophy of Aristotle, we have only attempted to indicate the lines upon which such resemblances may be traced. While in some cases there is a fair presumption for a direct connexion of thought or form of speech, in others there may be none. Much must be left to our judgement on other grounds.

It was reserved, in the fullness of time, for a people trained in the desert, and domiciled in Canaan, to have consummated amongst them that Gospel, in which "all that is imperishable in the moral philosophy of Greece lives on for

[1] Rom. ii. 14, 15.

ever." A people unphilosophical in all their habits and thoughts, and yet, by contact and communion with the One and the True, taught to know as axiomatic truths those things which the Greek thinker, approaching from the opposite standpoint of reason and induction, only with great labour attained to the conception of, and that imperfectly and with faltering apprehension.

(7) But we proceed to glance at that school of philosophy which in New Testament times was better known and more living than its predecessors, deriving its vitality from its practical character and the spirit of the age—Stoicism, as reflected in the New Testament.

The Synoptic Gospels represent the first simple recognition of the Christ, as He appeared among His own people, and lived, and acted, and taught; and they give the first pure Christian Ethics.

And it is here that Stoicism touches the early Christian teaching. There was an affinity already existing, owing to the fact that Stoicism had borrowed, or rather, owed much to, the spirit of Orientalism. "It was, in fact," says Bishop Lightfoot, in his exhaustive and interesting Essay on St. Paul and Seneca, "the earliest offspring of the union between the religious consciousness of the East and the intellectual culture of the West. The recognition of the claims of the individual soul, the sense of personal responsibility, the habit of judicial introspection, in short the subjective view of ethics were in no sense new, for they are known to have held sway over the mind of the chosen people from the earliest dawn of their history as a nation."

(8) In that lofty Beatitude of the Sermon on the Mount (St. Matt. v. 8), " Blessed are the pure in heart, for they shall see God," the reader is reminded of a saying of Seneca, not unlike— " The mind, unless it is pure and holy, comprehends not God [1]."

This is a striking coincidence. But, as Lightfoot has taken pains to show, while it is impossible to assign any real connexion between many of these parallels, it is not impossible to believe that in " Caesar's Court " the sayings of the Christians' Master may have subsequently penetrated, and many Christian maxims been found in circulation, so as even to reach the Stoic Seneca. At the same time he warns us to remember that in spirit Christianity and Stoicism were opposed, and that the context often changes the at first apparent drift of the pagan expression.

And it is inconceivable that the Prophet of Nazareth in any way borrowed from pagan philosophy. If the principal Stoic teachers came

[1] *Ep. Mor.* lxxxvii. 21.

from the East, it is not surprising that a resemblance should exist between their ethical teaching, so far as it went, and the expressions of religious thought familiar to Palestine. In the parallels, a few of which we now adduce, the Christian forms were almost certainly the earliest.

With regard to the sixth Beatitude, it occurs in the midst of others the spirit of which is in direct contrast with the human pride of Stoicism. The first alone, "Blessed are the poor in spirit," commences a line of thought utterly at variance with Stoical teaching.

And the blessedness of the "pure in heart" finds its parallel far back in Plato himself, who contended that the true exercise of a philosophical mind and habit, and a life corresponding to the greatness of the object sought, is the only road to the true sight and blissful enjoyment of the Good [1].

In any case, both Plato and Seneca only indicate a fact which is and must be true. But the deep spirituality and the personal sense of God that is the very life of the teaching of Christ, lifts the Beatitude on to another plane. And the vision of Ideas in the conception of Plato, possible only to the philosopher, denies the highest happiness to the poor and simple, who are on the other hand directly blessed in

[1] Comp. Wisdom i. 2-4; ix. 13-17.

the system of Christ, and with regard to the Beatific Vision.

With Plato, the soul was in its highest grade of activity by intellectually *knowing*; with Philo, by consideration of itself, shut off from the world [1]; with Seneca, by moral rectitude; with Christ, by spiritual reverence and love, and the death of self.

(9) The warnings of Christ against murder in the heart, and adultery in the thoughts, and the wisdom of cutting off the hand or plucking out the eye, find a parallel in Seneca's *de Benef.* v. 14, "A man is a robber even before he stains his hands; for he is already armed to slay, and has the desire to spoil and to kill;" and in his *Ep. Mor.* li. 13, "Cast out whatsoever things rend thy heart: nay, if they could not be extracted otherwise, thou shouldst have plucked out thy heart itself with them [2]."

(10) Matt. v. 44 is paralleled by "I will be agreeable to friends, gentle and yielding to enemies [3];" "Give aid even to enemies [4];" but the Stoic plainly falls short of the extreme demands following the "Love your enemies" of Christ and His apostle.

[1] *Migrat. Abr.* 34. 5.; *Somn.* i. 10; *de Abr.* 16.
[2] But see above, on Aristotle's *Ethics*.
[3] *De Vit. Beat.* 20.
[4] *De Otio*, 28. 1; and compare St. Paul in Rom. xii. 19-21.

(11) Matt. vi. 3: "When thou doest alms," &c.—"One ought to give so that another may receive. It is not giving or receiving to transfer to the right hand or to the left [1]."

(12) Matt. vi. 16: "When ye fast, be not as the hypocrites," &c.—"Do not, like those whose desire is not to make progress, but to be seen, do anything to attract notice in your demeanour or mode of life. Avoid a rough exterior and unshorn hair," &c.[2]

In such resemblances as these, we must remember that the Stoics had their Pharisees, their pretenders, even as the Jews, and that the sincere among them were constantly indignant at the unreality of their sham disciples.

(13) Our Lord, in Matt. xxiii. 27, likens the hypocrites of His time to whited sepulchres, beautiful outwardly, but corrupt within. Seneca has, "Within is no good; . . . where they are concealed, they are filthy, vile, adorned without, like their own walls," &c.[3]

Similarly, there are striking parallels to the parables of the Vine and the Branches, the Sower, the Talents, &c.

Some have even ventured to compare the "Father, forgive them" of the Cross, with Seneca's "There is no reason why thou shouldest

---

[1] *De Benef.* v. 8.   [2] *Ep. Mor.* v. 1. 2.
[3] *De Prov.* 6.

be angry; pardon them; they are all mad[1]." But the comparison is quite unworthy; one is the cry of the sublimest love; the other of the superiority of contempt.

(14) St. James (iv. 13) warns us not to be confident of the morrow, and suggests a pious "If the Lord will." Seneca says that the wise man will say, "I will sail unless anything happen, ... and, My business will turn out well for me unless anything happen[2]."

(15) Also, St. John's "Perfect love casteth out fear," is not unlike "Love cannot be mingled with fear[3]." And St. Peter's "Gird up the loins of your mind," resembles "Let the mind stand ready girt," &c.[4] See also St. Paul on the Christian armour in Eph. vi.

But while the Christian Scriptures urge these duties and mental attitudes as binding upon the *children of God*, Seneca is only advising the calm unruffled life of the man who would "do well unto himself."

(16) It is in St. Paul that the far larger number of coincidences are to be found. Many of them are certainly remarkable.

The passage, for instance, in Rom. i. 23— they "changed the glory of the incorruptible God into an image like to corruptible man," &c.

---

[1] *De Benef.* v. 17.
[2] *De Tranq. Anim.* 13.
[3] *Ep. Mor.* xlvii. 18.
[4] *Ad Polyb.* 11.

Seneca has, "They consecrate the holy and immortal and inviolable gods in motionless matter of the vilest kind; they clothe them with the forms of men, and beasts, and fishes[1]."

This however is but the statement of a fact which both apostle and philosopher would look upon with sorrow and scorn.

(17) So again, Rom. i. 28, 32—the "vile affections" and the "reprobate mind." Seneca speaks of their being enamoured of their evil deeds, and of their wretchedness being complete when they delight in and approve of shameful things[2].

(18) There is something higher in his "Pertinacious good overcomes evil men[3]," answering to Rom. xii. 21, "Be not overcome of evil, but overcome evil with good."

(19) But we need not enumerate here. Suffice it to point out the likeness of *spirit* in such sentences as "To obey God is liberty," with "Where the Spirit of the Lord is, there is liberty[4]."

(20) "Non licet plus effere quam intuleris[5]," "Abstulit (fortuna) sed dedit[6]." And 1 Tim. vi. 7: "For we brought nothing into the world, neither may we carry anything out." But probably St. Paul's parallel is with Job i. 21.

[1] *De Superst.* Frag. 31.
[2] *Ep. Mor.* xxxix. 6.
[3] *De Benef.* vii. 31.
[4] 2 Cor. iii. 17.
[5] *Ep. Mor.* cii. 25.
[6] *Ib.* lxiii. 7.

(21) More to the point is what we find in the history of the apostle's encounter with representatives of the Stoic school of his day, when in the Areopagus he was surrounded by both Stoics and Epicureans. Here are evidently [1] designed allusions on the part of St. Paul, who always adapted his teaching to his audience. He speaks of the Creator of the world, the Lord of heaven and earth, as "dwelling not in temples made with hands." His hearers would know that "the whole world was the temple of the immortal gods [2]," and that "Temples are not to be built to God of stones piled up on high [3]." If He is not "served with men's hands as though He needed anything," they were alive to the conviction that "God wants not ministers . . . He himself ministereth to the human race." If "He be not far from every one of us," they too confessed that "He is at hand everywhere and to all men [4]." "God is near thee. He is with thee; He is within [5]." And if we "ought not to think that He is like unto silver, or gold, or stone," &c.—they would admit that "they might not form Him of silver and gold, that no true likeness could be moulded thus [6]."

(22) But St. Paul touched them with a nearer

---

[1] Acts xvii. 22-31.
[2] Sen. *de Benef.* vii. 7.
[3] Fragm. 123.
[4] *Ep. Mor.* xcv. 47.
[5] *Ib.* xli. 1.
[6] *Ib.* xxxi. 11.

ETHICAL TRACES. 117

allusion still. One of their own poets was summoned as a witness, no other than Cleanthes, Zeno's disciple, whose noble hymn to Zeus contained the very words he was urging:

> "Thee
> 'Tis meet that mortals call with one accord,
> For we thine offspring are;"

unless indeed the apostle was thinking of another Stoic singer, his own countryman, Aratus of Tarsus, whose words,

> "And all in all things need we help of Zeus,
> For we too are his offspring,"

make the assertion in even exacter parallel.

But the apostle had prefaced his address with a reference to the altar with the strange inscription, Ἀγνώστῳ Θεῷ.—Research seems to show that this was not one of those altars to "an unknown god" mentioned by Pausanias, which would really be without a name; but rather a bona-fide confession that there is One God unknown and *unknowable*. Plutarch mentions a parallel inscription at Sais, giving it in Greek. Or there is the Ostian altar to Mithras, inscribed "Signum indeprehensibilis Dei." Mithraic or Sun-worship prevailed in the Roman world during the early Empire. Some such feeling, in the mixed and polytheistic worship of Athens, was doubtless expressed on the altar which the apostle so skilfully took for his text, leading the minds of his hearers, through the highest thoughts of their own prophets, to a conception of the Infinite Deity whom he was there to declare.

(23) "It is difficult," says Lightfoot, "to estimate, and perhaps not very easy to overrate, the extent to which Stoic philosophy had leavened the moral vocabulary of the civilized world at the time of the Christian era." And he instances the term συνείδησις, conscientia, "the most important of moral terms, the crowning triumph of ethical nomenclature." The idea of Conscience, we have seen, is traceable to Aristotle; but the term which expresses it is not derived from him. This, Lightfoot continues, "if not struck in the mint of the Stoics, at all events became current coin through their influence. To a great extent therefore the general diffusion of Stoic language would lead to its adoption by the first teachers of Christianity; while at the same time in St. Paul's own case personal circumstances might have led to a closer acquaintance with the diction of this school."

(24) Similarly, though the thought of an ideal citizenship is traceable to Aristotle and Plato, the language of the Stoic Seneca illustrates how the conception had become popularized and made familiar. "We are members of a vast body,"

he says; "Nature made us kin[1]." He speaks of two commonwealths; the one vast and truly called common, the boundaries of which are those set by the sun; and the other, that to which we are born by our nearer circumstances[2]. And again: "Nature bids me assist *men*; and whether they be bond or free, whether gentlefolk or freedmen, . . . what matter[3]?"

"Here again," says Lightfoot, "though the images are the same, the idea is transfigured and glorified. At length the bond of coherence, the missing principle of universal brotherhood, has been found. . . . The magic words ἐν Χριστῷ have produced the change and realized the conception. A living soul has been breathed into the marble statue by Christianity; and thus from the much-admired polity of Zeno arises the *Civitas Dei* of St. Augustine."

And if man in his corporate capacity is thus like and yet unlike in the Christian and the Stoic conception, so man in his individual responsibility, in his separate and personal independence, is a contrast indeed in the two systems. Again, in language and diction so like, but in meaning so unlike, St. Paul cries to the Corinthians, in whom the Stoic pride and arrogance

---

[1] *Ep. Mor.* xcv. 52.   [2] *De Otio*, 4, 31.
[3] *De Vit. Beat.* 24. Compare St. Paul, as above, Phil. iii. 20; Eph. ii. 16, &c.; Phil. i. 27, &c.

were not dormant or undeveloped, with doubtless a designed rebuke in the irony which does not hide the intense earnestness of his words, "Already ye are filled, already ye are become rich, ye have reigned as kings without us. . . . We are fools for Christ's sake, but ye are wise in Christ; we are weak, but ye are strong; ye are glorious, but we are dishonoured[1]." Similarly, in his Second Epistle he speaks more calmly of the Christian's wealth in Christ: "grieved, yet ever rejoicing; beggars, yet enriching many; possessors of nothing, and yet possessors of all things[2];" and "Always having all self-sufficiency (αὐτάρκειαν) in everything[3];" and "In whatsoever state I am, therein self-sufficing. . . . Able for everything in Him that strengtheneth me[4]." In those last words lie the secret, the contrast. The Stoic "Wise Man" professed to be all this, simply and alone in himself. He is all-sufficient; he wants for nothing: he possesses everything. He only of all men is free, he only is happy, he only is absolutely rich. To him alone appertains the true kinship and priesthood[5].

The Christian is all this; but not in himself. It is ἐν Χριστῷ, ἐν τῷ ἐνδυναμοῦντι that he takes

---

[1] 1 Cor. iv. 8, 10.   [2] 2 Cor. vi. 10.
[3] 2 Cor. ix. 8, 11.   [4] Phil. iv. 11-13.
[5] Seneca, *de Benef.* vii. 3, 4, 6, 10; *Ep. Mor.* ix. &c.

his stand and is more than conqueror, even in extreme adversity; "the exceeding greatness of the power is of God, and not from ourselves[1]." Because, as he had affirmed at the beginning, when showing how the true σοφία is found in the μωρία of God, "*All* things are yours; ye are Christ's, and Christ is God's[2]."

As Stoicism is the latest of the philosophical schools which we find influencing the language of the New Testament, owing to the peculiar circumstances of the age, so it also forms a link with the remaining portion of our subject—the traces of Roman law in the same Scriptures. There is one idea which, standing out strongly in St. Paul, in a passage already referred to, is discoverable both in Greek philosophy and Roman law; and which the Stoics took up and made popular. It is that of a law of Nature, distinct from and greater than the conventional usages of different lands and various ages. We shall have something to say about it presently; for it is difficult to think that St. Paul, himself a Roman citizen, did not use the term as from that standpoint; but at the same time it seems to have been really adopted from a philosophical source by the jurists of the Empire, who were "familiar with the training of the schools." They had their own way of deriving it, no

[1] 2 Cor. iv. 7-11, 16-18.   [2] 1 Cor. iii. 22, 23.

doubt; beneath the praetors' edicts they discovered rudiments of a law of nations which would itself suggest a primal law of Nature[1]. But there was doubtless some influence of the Stoic theory in this. And thus Christianity, as it gathered up the best and highest thoughts of the Greek philosophy, and breathed " a larger and humaner spirit " into the civil law, embraced in its wideness of universal truth and in its energy of appeal to the hearts and consciences of all men, all that was true and potent in each of these old world powers; and what "law could not do," and philosophy in its abstraction and want of a religion could not accomplish, Christianity stepped in and was able to take up, from its vantage-ground of an organized Society, inspired with a great Personal idea and burning with an enthusiastic zeal of individual and united service. The God that philosophy had felt after had revealed Himself, and a higher law had stepped in to supersede all laws of earth, and to bring about an eternal order of justice and right by the Νόμος τοῦ Πνεύματος τῆς ζωῆς ἐν Χριστῷ Ἰησοῦ, who was at the same time ὁ Λόγος, τὸ φῶς τὸ ἀληθινόν, ἐρχόμενον εἰς τὸν κόσμον.

[1] See p. 133.

ROMAN LAW.

VIII.

Roman Law at the Christian Era.

If there are traces of Greek philosophy in the New Testament, it is no less interesting to observe the influence exercised by Roman law upon the language and teaching of the Gospel of Jesus Christ. In one sense, that influence may be deemed even more important, as being more direct. For in the Epistles of St. Paul the principles of Roman law are brought in with so obvious a design and purpose, that without some acquaintance with those principles as applying in his day, it is impossible to follow closely his arguments and illustrations. A flood of light is thrown upon some of his closest theological trains of thought by remembering that as St. Paul was the principal formulator of Christian doctrine, as it has passed on to the Church, he was at the same time especially the interpreter of the Gospel to the Gentile nations, τοῖς βαρβάροις, who were not necessarily, though Greek-speaking, Greek in their modes of thought. The foundations of Hebraism were in many cases lacking; the philosophy of Greece in its deeper and more abstract forms might be little known; but the constant sense of that which penetrated the daily life of all who lived under the sway and dominion of the Roman Empire, the "citizenship" which was a practical reality, and not a mere social distinction; was a groundwork upon which the apostle, who was himself a Roman citizen, was able at once to approach the thoughts of his readers, and to construct the edifice of consistent and logical Christian teaching. This citizenship, this atmosphere of law, affected every relation of life. In daily business, in the payment of taxes, in the making of contracts, in the details of common domestic life, in disposing of property by will, or in succeeding to inheritances, the Roman was continually reminded of his "status," which differentiated him from all who were not enfranchised. His citizenship could not remain as an unheeded element of his everyday life. It was not a mere matter for the lawyers; for the jurisconsults were rather *professors* of law; and the private citizen must know his own privileges for himself, and so live his free and honoured life.

It will be a briefer task to indicate the traces of Roman law in view of our present purpose; for while the Greek philosophy, where discernible in the New Testament, was the reflection of a power in thought whose golden age was long past, and a possession arrived at through many channels and moderated by many strange influences, the civil law was in the early part of its golden era. It was a contemporary force in daily life. It was a voice ever at the back. It found a ready echo in the innate consciousness of the man himself, as well as in the principles enunciated in the religion of the One true Lawgiver, who was at once the Father and the Redeemer of the human family.

And an innate genius for law distinguished the Roman people. The science of jurisprudence was to them the intellectual life that the older philosophy was to the Greek. And St. Paul, in speaking as a Roman to Romans, was really casting Christian theology into a practical philosophical form which would appeal to the Church of future centuries with a power that the abstract, metaphysical thinking of the more profound Greek mind would fail to yield, so far as regarded the mass of men whose lives were to be moulded and influenced thereby. It might ever be a matter of dispute what Plato or Aristotle, in this or that teaching or writing, had really said or really meant; with what precise shade of meaning, or exactly with what intent, St. John used the historical term Logos, and whether with him it was more Hebraic than Philonean; but St. Paul's "Know ye not? For I speak to them that know the Law," which frequently expressed the spirit of his teaching both as a Roman and as a Jew, was definite and direct, and left the reader only one course—to apply the lesson to his practical conduct and belief.

Except among the Jews of Palestine, what has just been said would generally hold good. There, the case was not quite the same. Rome conquered and governed Judaea, but it was not made a Roman colony or subjected to Roman law. But elsewhere the Roman law touched closely the lives of its vast multitudes of subjects, and the apostle of the Gentiles would be well understood in his allusions and arguments, so full of force from the circumstances of the day in which he lived, and from the authority with which, as a "civis Romanus," he could urge them.

But though St. Paul is the principal exponent of the message and service which Roman law had to render to the Divine truth, it is not in his writings alone that such traces are to be found. Scattered here and there, even in the

Gospels, allusions may be discovered; and in the Epistle to the Hebrews, thus perhaps showing the influence of St. Paul, even though we do not accept it as coming from his pen, there is a very striking example of analogical teaching from the civil law. And in the Acts of the Apostles we see how the very progress of the [infant Church was greatly assisted and protected by the establishment everywhere of the Roman power, and the respect to Roman rights. Thus, as the atmosphere of Roman legalism surrounded the brief career of the Founder of Christianity from His birth to His death,

"Imperante Augusto, natus est Christus; imperante Tiberio crucifixus;"

His birth in Bethlehem being the result of the requirements of the Roman census, His unjust delivery to death for our redemption the work of a Roman Procurator, terrified by an allusion to a Lex "de Majestate"; and its instrument, the Cross, the ever-remaining symbol of the Faith; so, when the work of the Christ on earth was ended, the same power became the nursing-mother to the Faith as it grew and spread into all lands, and a vehicle for its profoundest doctrines as they were brought to bear upon the Roman world.

It will help us to take a brief glance at some of the leading features of Roman law, which lent themselves so readily to the analogical uses which we shall presently consider.

Roman law was rich in principle, logical exactness, and scientific method.

The provisions and institutions of the civil law as relating to persons (one of the three great divisions as later on classified by Gaius) were important and peculiar.

Persons were either freemen or slaves. This fundamental distinction will be seen to offer many thoughts of value to the Christian teacher.

(1) The first idea as touching freemen, is that of the citizen. He was possessed of a civil personality, called his "caput," which was possessed of special rights, privileges, and duties. This personality or "persona" was detachable in thought from the man himself. It expressed the sum total of his rights and duties. It might be lost or forfeited, by what was called "capitis deminutio," which affected his position as a free man, a citizen, or a member of the family. Though living, he might become civilly dead. His "caput" involved all that was dear to him in the concerns and interests of daily life.

(2) Then there was the law of the family. The Patria Potestas, peculiar to the Romans, was a most important element in their social system, and full of suggestiveness with regard to the

lessons to be drawn from Christian doctrine; and, as we shall see, by no means left out of account by St. Paul. Sir Henry Maine, in his *Ancient Law* [1], maintains that it was the " nidus " out of which the entire law of persons germinated. By it the Roman father possessed most sweeping rights and powers over all the members of his household, including his agnatic descendants and slaves. Even the wife, or mother of the family, held only the position of an adopted daughter. His children possessed nothing of their own; all that they earned was their father's. If they had injured any one, they might be delivered over bodily to the injured party; they might be sold, and the pater-familias held the "jus vitae necisque."

(3) Closely connected with this was the law of adoption. This was an important and prominent feature of Roman law. By it the family might be legally extended. The adopted son was as truly and really representative of his adoptive father, for all purposes of succession, as a son born in the "matrimonium justum." The adopted son took a higher place than mere blood relations. The " familia " depended on the " agnatic " group, and the merely cognatic were ignored. Supposing there were no male heir, by adoption or arrogation the desired end could at once be

[1] P. 182.

accomplished. The person thus brought into the family assumed the family name, "partook in its mystic sacrificial rites, and became, not on sufferance or at will, but to all intents and purposes, a member of the house of his adopter; nor could the tie thus formed be broken save through the ceremony of emancipation." His former personality was extinguished and dead. If he had been "sui juris," his old debts could no longer be charged against him. And so complete was the change that had taken place, that intermarriage between the newly formed relations was as strictly forbidden as if they had been related by blood.

The Pauline phraseology, which incorporates the beautiful metaphor of adoption, is one of the most important examples, as reflecting the influence of Roman law on theology and devotion, of the connexion which has to be pointed out between that source of ideas and imagery and the form which New Testament teaching has taken. Adoption, in the Roman sense, has no place in our laws, nor any very definite one in our customs. In a legal sense, moreover, it was not known to the Jews. Fictitious kinship was not traced in their genealogies.

(4) The law of succession and inheritance is another important feature. Theoretically, the heir stepped at once into all the rights and

responsibilities of the deceased. He became clothed in his "persona." "The notion was that though the physical person of the deceased had perished, his legal personality survived and descended unimpaired to his heir or co-heirs, in whom his identity (so far as the law was concerned) was continued[1]." "The testator lived on in his heir, or in the group of his co-heirs. He was in law the same person with them[2]." "In pure Roman jurisprudence the principle that a man lives in his heir—*the elimination, so to speak, of the fact of death*—is too obviously for mistake the centre round which the whole law of testamentary and intestate succession is circling[3]." This fact may be traced back to the period when the family, not the individual, was the unit of society.

Although English law contains the maxim, "Nemo est heres viventis," this principle did not obtain among the Romans. A child was his father's heir from the day of his birth. "Heres" meant lord or proprietor. "The namesake of the apostle, Paul the jurist, who lived in the third century after Christ, observes that there is a species of co-partnership in the family property between a father and his children; 'When, therefore,' says he, 'the father dies, it is not so

---

[1] Maine, *Ancient Law*, p. 181. [2] *Ib.* p. 188.
[3] *Ib.* p. 190.

correct to say that they succeed to his property, as that they acquire the free control of their own.' This inchoate partnership of an unemancipated son in his father's possessions, and his close identification with his person, may be regarded as some set-off against the quasi-servitude of his position under the formidable 'patria potestas [1].'"

All this becomes extremely important when considering some of St. Paul's most powerful pleadings and arguments with Christians to remember and live up to their privileges as "heirs of God."

(5) The Roman law of testamentary succession, and of contract, will be found of special interest with regard to one important passage, at least, in the New Testament.

(6) And the law of guardianship, tutorship, &c., as connected with the patria potestas and the care of property, again supplies apostolic teaching with language and force.

(7) The marriage of the Romans, too, in the early days of the state, was a matter of great strictness, and the idea of "the one man and the one woman" was remarkable. The passing into the "manus," or power of her husband, was a prominent feature. We cannot say that St. Paul, in speaking to Romans [2], had not this in mind

[1] W. E. Ball, LL.D. [2] Rom. vii.

quite as much as the marriage code of the Jews.

Other features less prominent will meet us incidentally as we examine the New Testament.

(8) The law of Nature here claims a remark.

The "Jus Naturale" belonged to the primary definitions and divisions of law [1]. In the history of law as well as of theology it plays a considerable part. As connected with civil jurisprudence, it is exclusively Roman. Here Cicero and St. Paul, old philosophy and later legalism, stand on common ground in many respects. Later and modern philosophy, too, has taken it up. Conscience in the man, equity in the law, the progress of jurisprudence and legislation, as well as of private and national ethics, and moral theories of republican reformers and philosophers, have drawn liberally upon the noble idea of Nature's law, though its significance and meaning may have been widely different in the various cases.

"The ancient Quiritarian law, elaborately ceremonial in its character, was regarded as the peculiar heritage of the Roman citizen. Foreigners were jealously excluded from participating in its benefits. A separate system and separate tribunals were established for those who were outside the pale of citizenship. Every

---

[1] So Gaius, and after him Justinian.

student of Roman law knows how this subsidiary system, distinguished for its extreme simplicity and based on reason instead of immemorial usage, was gradually brought into competition with the old Quiritarian jurisprudence, and finally superseded it. Originally disliked and despised, the Praetorian law, by means in part of the Stoical philosophy, came to be the object of peculiar admiration. It was lauded as the law of Nature, restored from the golden age; it was eulogized by the name of equity [1]."

And with the Roman lawyers the "Jus Gentium" was often confounded with this law of Nature, and called by the same name. "The wider the Roman dominion spread, the wider became the views of their jurists; and in this way arose the notion of a law common to the Romans with other nations, and with all mankind [2]."

When we come to look at some of the interesting passages in St. Paul where, as we have already intimated, he draws upon his familiarity with Roman law, the importance of the principles and theories above indicated will be fully seen.

[1] W. E. Ball, LL.D.   [2] Phillimore, *Roman Law*, p. 24.

IX.

ROMAN LAW AND THE PROGRESS OF THE EARLY CHURCH [1].

THE dominion of Rome was a protection and help to the progress of the Gospel in its earliest days. The widespread peace and the established authority that prevailed were significant, among other preparatory elements of the age, of the fact that "the fullness of the time was come." More than this, the idea was made possible to men's conceptions of a universal allegiance to a throne and a power, which enabled them to grasp the central thought of Christianity, in their worship of "another king, one Jesus." The civilized world of that date was under one dominant system of law; ease and safety of travel and communication between distant places was assured; the way was opened up for the spread

---

[1] Professor Ramsay's new and interesting book, *St. Paul the Traveller and Roman Citizen*, has only come into my hands since going to press, and too late for use. It should be carefully read. I have added a footnote or two.

of that dominion which should claim obedience from all nations. The crooked places were made straight, and the rough places plain [1].

St. Paul, the great ambassador to the Gentile world of this new and sovereign power, was specially fitted for his peculiar work. He was a "civis Romanus" by birth [2], though a Jew by education and religion. He was thus fitted to be the messenger of the Faith to men of both nations. Brought up under the "potestas" of his father, his character would be specially fitted and formed for his work among those of the Roman nationality, or those who dwelt under its wide rule. The habits of discipline and strength of character thus imbibed, would stand him in good stead when his turn came for severe and trying endurance and action, for organizing, ruling, and guiding the infant community he was to do so much to form. His citizenship would be the means of assisting him to carry the Gospel he taught wellnigh all over the known world, from the humblest "colonus" to the house-

---

[1] In v. 12 of his book Dr. Ramsay dwells on the Pauline use of "Ecclesia." He thinks the apostle transferred to this word the idea of the unified empire, "Rome." In the most distant province, a group of Roman citizens meeting together as a "conventus civium Romanorum," formed a part of the great conception, a fragment of "Rome." So the Church "in Corinth." The idea has its beauty, but perhaps should not be pressed.

[2] Acts xxii. 28.

hold of Caesar himself. At the same time, his Greek tongue and education would wing his utterances to the ears of the most cultivated and philosophical men of his day.

The Book of the Acts of the Apostles is full of instances of the advantage of St. Paul's Roman citizenship to him in his missionary work. In some cases it made persecution, always ready to follow him, difficult; in others, it refused to be made its instrument. The law which tolerated his own countrymen could not be bent to help their clamours when they wished to turn it against him. If the question was only one "of their law" or profession of faith, the Roman "would be no judge of such matters [1]."

The apostle commenced his great work from Antioch in Syria as a starting-point. As falling in with our present line of thought, it was well chosen for the purpose, as it was the seat of a peaceful Roman administration. It was here that the followers of the Galilean first received the name of Christiani, and the name was borne by them apparently unmolested [2].

Sergius Paulus, the Proconsul of Cyprus, was his first convert. From him the apostle received the name by which he was ever afterwards known. Was not this remarkable incident

---

[1] Acts xviii. 16.   [2] Acts xi. 26.

a foreshadowing of the intimate link of union that was to subsist ever afterwards between the Roman apostle " and all the peoples of the West," not merely in his own future struggles and victories for his Master, but down the centuries of the Christian life which was to distinguish the civilization of Europe? The pathway provided by the Empire was utilized and blessed for the progress of the Church [1].

St. Paul's possession of the "Jus Civitatis," and his standing as a Roman, comes out in an interesting passage in Acts xvi. 35-39. Philippi, a Roman military colony, was founded by Augustus under the high-sounding name of "Colonia Augusta Julia Philippensis." Upon it he conferred the privileges of the "Jus Italicum."

There was a difference between the colony and the municipal city: the former " was a reproduction, as far as possible, of the capital itself;" the latter was formed more on the pattern of the old Italian communities. But in both a higher conception of the honour of citizenship, and the value that attached to it, prevailed, than was the case in the Mother City

---

[1] On "Saul" and "Paul," see Ramsay, ii. 1 and iv. 4, on the twofold personality possible in the political and bi-lingual life of that day. After Acts xiii. 9, the subordinate "Saul" gives place to the pioneer "Paul."

herself. There slaves were sometimes emancipated in crowds in order to gratify a wealthy testator's vanity by sending forth these witnesses to his liberality at the expense of his heir. Thus the franchise became degraded, and consequently less esteemed [1]. It was not so in such places as we are now considering, nor where St. Paul found it necessary to claim his rights as a Roman citizen.

At Philippi the apostle's preaching was the means of bringing about a dispute and disturbance concerning a slave. The owners of the damsel " possessed with a spirit of Python " had apparently made much gain out of their unhappy property by trading on the superstitions and credulities of the people. The Divine power, acting through St. Paul, released the victim from her spiritual thraldom. She would henceforth be of no more use to her masters. Paul and Silas therefore were dragged straightway before the magistrates, and the damage done to a slave, for which there was a remedy at law, became the occasion for persecution and hasty action on the part of the Praetors. Without listening to any defence they roughly committed the Christian teachers to prison, after disgracing them by public scourging. But on the arrival of the

[1] In A. D. 8 the "Lex Furia Caninia" was made expressly to check this wild use of the right of manumission.

"lictores" with the message to dismiss the prisoners, the apostle made a wise and spirited use of his privileges as a Roman citizen. They were, he protested, "indemnati," uncondemned. They had been treated with violence as being Christians. But there was more to be said. "Romani" they were also[1]. They claimed at the hands of the magistrates not only recognition, but protection from insult, as a matter of right. The Praetors themselves, on the other hand, were liable to no small punishment for this violation on their part of the Porcian laws. The effect was immediate. The Duumvirs came to the prisoners in person and humbly admitted the wrong. Henceforward greater care would be exercised that Roman citizens were not lightly ill-treated.

St. Paul was really a citizen of Tarsus. According to Pliny it was neither a Roman colony nor a "municipium," but an "urbs libera." So that (as see also in ch. xxii. 29) his "civitas," which saved him later from another scourging, must have been acquired in some other way, perhaps through an ancestor who had been

---

[1] This statement, echoing the very words of their accusers (xvi. 21), was startling to the *strategi*. In Cicero's charges against Verres, the heaviest of all was the breach of this law: "*Facinus est vinciri civem Romanum, scelus verberari*" (Cic. in Verr. v. 57). See Ramsay, x. 5.

presented with his freedom for some service rendered to the Roman Emperor [1].

We pass on to another instance. At Thessalonica, where the apostle made a great step forward in his missionary work by the founding of a Church, he found himself in a free Roman city. Under the Roman Empire, Thessalonica became the capital of one of the four governments of Macedonia; and later on, when they were united, the metropolis. The city was the principal station on the Via Egnatia, or highroad to Rome from the countries lying north of the Aegean. Thus it was a centre of great advantage for the spread of the new faith. "Here was a synagogue of the Jews," who were largely drawn hither by commerce. The Church founded here by St. Paul became of considerable importance, and for several centuries a bulwark of Christianity in the East. The constitution of the city was interesting. Jason and certain of the brethren were brought ἐπὶ τοὺς πολιτάρχους, for harbouring the messengers of the Christian faith. These politarchs presided

[1] On St. Paul's citizenship, Prof. Ramsay, in *St. Paul the Traveller* (ii. 1), says, "It is probable, but not certain, that the family had been planted in Tarsus with full rights as part of a colony settled there by one of the Seleucid kings in order to strengthen their hold on the city." That the citizenship was presented to his father for some service to the state he thinks less probable.

over the Demos, or popular assembly. Though an apparently Greek city, the apostle found here an open door for the successful spread and establishment of the one true religion.

As Pilate had given Christ over to the people's will from terror at their cry, "If thou let this man go, thou art not Caesar's friend!" so here in Thessalonica a charge of treason under the laws "De Majestate" was brought against the Christians. They were accused of saying that there was "another king, one Jesus." The person of the emperor had become substituted for the dignity of the people at large, which was the real meaning of Cicero's "majestas est quaedam magnitudo populi Romani." The crime of majestas, defined by Ulpian as being "adversus populum Romanum," was now easily committed by simply "speaking against Caesar."

But the disturbance caused by the envious Jews was not responded to by the politarchs, except so far as to take the "satisdatio" of Jason and those with him.

Following the apostle to Berea, we find him again pursued by his relentless persecutors; and being here outside the protection of Roman law, the brethren felt it a wiser course to hasten the apostle forward to Athens.

In ch. xviii an incident full of interest comes before us. The Proconsul of Corinth was

Annaeus Novatus Gallio, the brother of Seneca. He appears to have been a lawyer of enlightened views and integrity of character. The Jews here made "insurrection" against Paul, and preferred a religious charge against him. He "was persuading men to worship God contrary to their law." That is, that while they, the Jews, were permitted by the Roman law to worship God according to the law of Moses, the Christians were to be condemned and punished for not following them. Judaism was a "religio licita;" but Christianity, not yet the object of persecution by edict, was, by this accusation, made an offence at least against the public peace. The accusers were, however, disappointed. Gallio, following the policy of the Roman governors generally, not to interfere in mere religious disputes, would not recognize the offence, contemptuously ignoring even the act of violence before the judgement seat ; and thus the law became a shield of protection to the growing Church, though in this instance only in a negative way.

In the next chapter St. Paul is at Ephesus, where again the Roman law is his protection. Ephesus was the capital of the Roman proconsular province of Asia. The city was a free one. Its laws and constitution came in as a strong protecting power to the help of the apostle in his mission. His work had, by its continued success, raised vehement opposition. Ephesus was an assize town, and (verse 38) the court was actually open at the time, and the proconsuls ready to administer justice. The town-clerk addressed the multitude in a speech of great sense and tact; and the fear of forfeiting their rights acted at once upon them as a powerful antidote to the spirit of riot and disorder, and again the apostle of the Gentiles was permitted to go free.

In the twenty-second chapter St. Paul is again claiming the privilege and immunity of a citizen of Rome, when threatened with examination by scourging by Claudius Lysias, the tribune. The simple question put by the apostle to the centurion was quite enough to fill the chief captain with fear. Nay, the mere fact that he had bound him was a source of misgiving; for the statement of the prisoner that he was a Romanus was the secret. The chief captain at once interviewed him personally. " Dic mihi, tu Romanus es?" The reply affirmed it. The tribune felt that his equal at least stood before him. " Ego multa pecunia civitatem hanc consecutus sum," was his astonished remark. Nay; but his astonishment was to be even greater. "Ego autem et natus sum," was the apostle's response. Then at once " qui eum torturi erant" departed from him. They dare not proceed. Claudius Lysias was himself only a "libertus" or freed-man. The victim of the popular displeasure was his superior even there. Immediately the apostle is accorded full protection, and escorted from Jerusalem to Caesarea to appear before Felix, to whom a letter is dispatched representing the seizure of the prisoner in a very different light from the bare facts.

At Caesarea the apostle is kept for two years in prison, after the first hearing of the case, through the unprincipled conduct of Felix the governor, himself only a freed-man of the Emperor Claudius. In defiance of the laws of which he was an administrator, he kept the accused in remand with a view of extorting money from him, thus rendering himself liable to the punishment of exile, which under the Empire followed a breach of the laws "De Pecuniis Repetundis." St. Paul, however, would not help him in this, any more than, later on, he would infringe the "Lex Fabia de Plagiariis," in the case of Onesimus, whom he restored to his master. But this unjust confinement of two years' duration became an opportunity for speaking his message before the governor and his friends, and must have borne good fruit in other ways. To curry favour with the Jews, however, Felix left him at the conclusion of his own term of office still a prisoner, and Porcius Festus succeeded as the guardian and protector of the great ambassador of the Kingdom of Heaven.

Thirsting for his life, the Jews had, on the eve of St. Paul's hasty journey under escort to Caesarea, formed a deadly plot against him, which was frustrated by the prompt action of Claudius Lysias. Now again (ch. xxv) we find them endeavouring to entrap the new governor into a course that would have gratified their malice by giving them an opportunity of slaying the apostle. Had Festus granted them the favour they asked, and sent for St. Paul to Jerusalem, he would have commenced his term of office by conciliating an influential section of the Jewish people; and doubtless there was some temptation to do this. But the spirit of integrity was strong enough in the new governor to withstand this; the prosecutors were ordered to go themselves to Caesarea, and the apostle was once more saved by the action of the Roman rule.

At the new trial at Caesarea, St. Paul availed himself of the privilege offered by the higher court, which had gradually grown up under the Empire, and "appealed unto Caesar." Here again he acted upon his rights as a Roman citizen, and the appeal apparently could not be disallowed by Festus. At the same time the fact of his having appealed prevented his being set at liberty, as, in consequence of the light thrown by Herod Agrippa II, as guardian of the Temple, on the local bearings of the case, he evidently would have been [1]. But from this time we trace him in easier circumstances. Greater honour is accorded him; more liberty is given him; until in the great centre and capital of the Empire we find him boldly and freely making known his world-wide message, and establishing a firm home for the Gospel in the seat of law and authority. He is now the apostle of the Gentiles in literal fact. "I would have you understand," he says, writing to the Philippians from Rome, "that the things which have happened unto me have fallen out rather unto the furtherance of the Gospel; so that my bonds become manifest in Christ throughout the whole praetorian guard, and to all the rest; and that most of the brethren in the Lord, being confident through my bonds, are more abundantly bold to speak the word of God without fear."

In such a way then, by the over-ruling hand of Providence, through the power of a greater dominion than that of Imperial Rome, was the great world-power of the age made subservient to the establishment of the Kingdom of the Christ, which in time should even take the place and utilize the organization of the ruling power which, after acting first as a cradle and protec-

[1] Acts xxvi. 32.

tion to the Church, should presently meet it face to face as a rival; and by-and-by bow down before it, and give it place. In doing this, it should impart to it something of its principles, system, and language, and so further the dominion of an international and spiritual state, of an eternal monarchy, which should demand and obtain the allegiance of all races of men.

The important part which the Roman Empire was destined to play, thus, in the spread of the Christian Faith, is shown to some extent by the facts and details above given. We shall also, by the glance now taken, have become familiarized with the atmosphere of Roman law in which the apostle St. Paul moved and taught. Without this aid and influence, it is probable that the Latin races and Western peoples would have in a great measure failed to receive and to assimilate the profound truths and conceptions of the Gospel. In the great Epistle to the Romans themselves they found the message adapted to them, and conveyed to them "in their own tongue wherein they were born." And in St. Paul's letters to the Corinthians and the Galatians many familiar images would occur to the minds of his readers in his earnest arguments concerning Christian privilege and duty, powerfully enforced by appeals to the laws so well understood in their general principles, and so apt in their details. The Gospels contain, of course, the statement of facts affecting our religion rather than the reasoning of doctrines; and this is sometimes urged in disparagement of theology as such, the important fact being overlooked that before the Faith could be taught its foundations must be laid. But the Epistles of St. Paul are indeed theological treatises. Abstract argument has a large place in them; Divine metaphysics are formulated into a system.

Christianity travelled from the East to the West; and though for the first two centuries it was still under the influence of Greek thought and the Greek tongue, the characteristics of the Roman spirit forbade that it should for a lengthened period be ruled by the influence of Greece. The philosophy which was reflected in the theology of the East, was represented in the West by the legal genius of the Roman Empire; and it is not to be denied that a powerful stamp has been given to modern Christianity by the mould of Roman law in which so many of its conceptions were cast. Christology is the distinctive theology of the Greek-speaking Church; Soteriology that of the Latin. The intellectual and speculative Eastern mind seized upon subtle metaphysical points, while the Western genius turned to practical questions of law and system, and of the making of a man "just with God."

Ready to the hand of the latter was the possession of a language and a habit of thought which enabled it to meet the questions of free-will and grace, of moral obligation, of transmitted sin or liability, of satisfaction and atonement, which never, in the same way, troubled the Eastern mind.

In tracing the influence of Roman law on the writings of the New Testament, we shall plainly see how all this holds good even with regard to the first approach of the truth to the Western mind.

X.

Allusions to Roman Law in the New Testament.

Before proceeding to the consideration of the extremely interesting and important use made by St. Paul of analogies and principles drawn from Roman law, a glance at some allusions, more or less striking, in other parts of the New Testament will appropriately come in here.

We meet with one or two in the Sermon on the Mount, among our Lord's most solemn and earnest exhortations. The figure used in St. Matt. v. 25 presents us with a picture of the proceedings in a civil suit, belonging in its outlines to the earliest days of Roman law. A debtor is called by his creditor to appear before the praetor, by the "in jus vocatio." The advice is given, ἴσθι εὐνοῶν τῷ ἀντιδίκῳ σου ταχύ, the ἀντίδικος being properly an opponent in a suit at law, though here the creditor. To settle the dispute "in the way" was a course by no means unknown; for the law allowed the "transactio in via" to close the matter, so that the defaulting party need not be dragged into court, where, an action being granted, a "judex" would be appointed, and the matter carried to the bitter end.

The parable of the insolvent debtor [1] contains an obvious reference to a practice under the Roman law, though possibly the imagery is coloured by some Oriental details. The command that the man was to be sold, "with his wife and children and all that he had," rested upon the assumption that they were part of his property, as by the Patria Potestas, and by the practice and theory of the Roman law, they would be. True, the Mosaic law permitted a similar sale, but under softening conditions; and by the time of our Lord it is more than probable that the custom had entirely disappeared from among the Jews. The imprisonment at least was not Jewish; while the cruelty of the laws of the Twelve Tables with regard to debtors is well known. The thirty days' grace; the imprisonment in irons; the threefold declaration of debt by the creditor; the doom of the sixtieth day; and the spirit of insatiate vengeance expressed in the final deprivation of liberty or life, form a background sufficiently dark for the picture before us.

The punishment of the debtor is of a nature

[1] Matt. xviii. 23-35.

derived from the conception of the family as a unit, represented by, and in the power of, the head, under the Patria Potestas.

These two instances simply touch the influence of the Roman administration upon the imagery and language of the New Testament. As we have before remarked, Palestine was not colonized by Rome; the law was only felt so far as the necessary sway of the Empire was exercised in its general authority and administration; yet we cannot help seeing that the popular conception of *sin*, in its relation to God, and the position and danger of the soul of man, together with the doctrine of eternal punishment, and the idea of the Atonement as a loosing from *debt*, or as an actual payment of a sum due to the Deity, &c.—conceptions prevalent even to-day, as well as in mediaeval and scholastic theology—have largely owed their expression to the language of these parables. To minds familiar with the legal ideas suggested, this result would be a natural one, more especially when we remember the proneness of men's minds to press symbolical language even beyond its legitimate force, of which the second of these parables has often been an example. For the cancelling of the money debt would be a complete transaction; and yet, here, the debt is charged again. Oriental despotism might sanction such a punishment, but higher notions of justice rebel. It is not to be denied that a great deal of European theology abounds with arguments, drawn from this and similar sources, which are only defensible upon the assumption of a sort of absolutism in the judge arising from a kind of deification of penal law. This very aptitude of the Western mind to "legalize" the language of Scripture beyond its intent shows how apt a vehicle for some of the great arguments concerning sin and atonement the imagery of law would prove to the apostle of the Gentiles. The moral of the parable of the unmerciful servant is undoubtedly that of the sin of a spirit of unforgiveness, which insists on its legal rights, "jus suum," forgetful of the fact of a free and gracious pardon received, and of the "jura domini" which had never been rendered.

Among the passing allusions in thought or language, which are to be found scattered throughout the New Testament, we note the passage in St. Matthew v. 41, referring to the assistance to the public courier which the government demanded. The origin of the custom was rather Persian than Roman; but the ὅστις σε ἀγγαρεύσει was not merely Latinized by the "Quicunque te angariaverit," but the very term would be familiar to a dweller in the Roman provinces of that day.

A very important illustration, drawn direct from Roman testamentary law, occurs in the Epistle to the Hebrews, ch. ix. 15-17.

This Epistle is so Hebrew in its general teaching and thought, and so Alexandrian in its style, that it might well be supposed we should hardly look here for allusions to Roman law. And yet, without reference to the Roman law of will-making, the explanation of the apparent confusion of thought between "covenant" and "testament," which has puzzled so many, cannot be satisfactorily found.

The word διαθήκη, which in the Authorized Version is translated sometimes "covenant" and sometimes "testament," is found thirty-three times in the New Testament. The Evangelists employ the term in their account of the institution of the Sacrament by our Lord at the Supper. "Covenant" is almost certainly the correct rendering in that connexion. At the same time the thought of death which overshadowed that solemn hour may suggest the will or testament of Him who was about to leave the world. But the passage in the Epistle to the Hebrews is an example of the real value of understanding something of the Roman will; and the argument, if not St. Paul's own, reflects most probably the influence of his mind in that famous scriptural treatise. It is important to remember here, and in connexion with the whole subject of testaments, that the will was peculiarly the invention of the Romans; and the Roman conquest was the occasion for the invention of the Rabbinical will, which was directly based upon the Roman.

The Roman will was originally a "contract." It was moreover a transaction not always involving the thought of immediate death. No writing was required. The contract itself was verbal. It was a means by which the man, yet living, could in the presence of witnesses secure to his heir after his death the property he stood possessed of. It necessarily differed from the modern idea of a will in being irrevocable; and also in being necessarily open. It was a contract " inter vivos," springing from the ancient " mancipium " or conveyance, which must be regarded as the real origin also of the modern contract. Both contract and will are thus traceable to the same source. It was by this conveyance by copper and scales that the early Roman secured the attainment of his wishes as we do now by the sealed will. Sir Henry Maine thinks it took effect at once, inasmuch as mancipation did not admit of " conditio " or " dies." But some civilians suppose there was a sort of understanding not to disturb the vendor as long as he lived. From the language of the passage before us this certainly seems probable as regards New Testament days. "A testament is of force after men are dead [1]."

Now with regard to the apparent confusion of terms. The argument has been on the bringing in of the New Covenant by Christ, in place of the Old Covenant established by Moses. That Old Covenant was sanctified and ratified by blood—by death. The thought passes by a rapid transition to the idea of a will or testament, the same word, connected in history and thought; and the "inheritance," just spoken of, completes the suggestion. Death comes in, in both cases. The points all agree. Christ brought in a New Covenant by His own blood. Christ at the same time left us an inheritance confirmed to us by His death. He left us a testament. And so the ancient conveyance "per aes et libram," which embraced the contract and will in one, and was not yet superseded by the praetorian will, though that was known from Cicero's time, serves to bring home to the reader's mind the sure mercies of redemption.

But the praetorian will, so called because founded on the praetor's *Edictum* or dispensing power, gradually superseded the old "mancipatio," especially in the provinces.

A vision in the Revelation of St. John, which

[1] Heb. ix. 17.

has its effect on the whole of the connected series of events in that remarkable prophecy, gives the representation of a Roll or Book, sealed with seven seals. It has been suggested [1] that this is nothing else than an image drawn from the praetorian will just mentioned, which must have been known to St. John, and to the readers of the Revelation. This will, when written, was witnessed and sealed sevenfold. It differed from the old "mancipatio" or sale, in that the contents were thus secret [2], and the *seven* witnesses attested the genuineness of the *document* [3], as opposed to the old *five* [4], who only attested the genuineness of the *act*. In Rev. v. 1 St. John represents, in the right hand of God

---

[1] By the Rev. E. H. Curwen, D.C.L., of Plumbland, Carlisle. The idea is here enlarged upon. On the subject of the Roman will, the reader may consult the article 'Testamentum' in Smith's *Dictionary of Antiquities*, second ed. p. 1113; or third ed. vol. ii. p. 803.

[2] Though it *might* be made "sine scriptis," as the old will *might* be written. But of course the image is that of the valid written will which, as a system, was used. Seals were not unknown before, but only now became legally requisite.

[3] The first appearance of sealing, as a necessary mode of authentication. The seals were "literally fastenings which had to be broken before the writing could be inspected." See Maine's *Ancient Law*, chap. vi.

[4] That is, five besides the *libripens* and the *familiae emptor*, who were necessary actors. The complete number seven held good in each.

the Father, a parchment roll, the Testament of His providential history and the expression of His purposes, "closed and sealed with seven seals." This imagery is very striking, and the very term used of the whole of the Gospel legacy, the "New Testament," seems to bear witness in its use to the legitimacy and the power of the illustration both here, and as made use of by the writer to the Hebrews.

Besides what has been said, it is worthy of notice that Christ is represented as the High Priest, as well as the Mediator of a new and better Testament to His Church. Thus the mingling of metaphors may not be so arbitrary as at first sight would appear. The heir of pagan Rome was also a hierophant. The institution of the will itself was probably due to the horror with which the ancient world regarded any neglect of the dead in respect of those duties which were the first functions of the heir. The Manes must be propitiated, and the departed and the survivors both looked, so to speak, to the heir to keep the communication between them unbroken. If ancestor-worship is wrapped up in this, it may at least point to the remains of a simpler primeval faith, in which the idea of the Fatherhood of God survived in that of the natural father. But the point is, that inheritance had an early sacerdotal aspect. And Christ is both High Priest and also "Surety" of the better Testament. Here is the Gospel in terms of the Roman law.

The few instances just brought forward, show us what an influence the language and thoughts of those early days has had upon the terminology and formation of our Christianity, and its expressions of belief. Whatever the road, the Truth would doubtless have reached us; but by the road on which we are now travelling, it meets us with realistic force [1].

[1] On Titus iii. 5, 1 Pet. iii. 21, Acts viii. 34-38, see pp. 180-182.

XI.

ROMAN LAW IN ST. PAUL'S EPISTLES.

IT has been pointed out, that there is a similarity between St. Paul's use of *Nomos* and Philo's use of *Logos*, as a voice or monitor in the human soul [1]. The Stoical law of nature, also, has been seen to have suggested much to the Roman jurists which they expressed in their Praetorian law. In the Epistle to the Romans we find St. Paul contrasting the law of Moses, or of legal and moral obligation, with the law of the Spirit of Life in Christ Jesus.

In all this we may reasonably believe that there is a thread of connected thought, undesigned, it may truly be, but still traceable.

There is a sort of similar movement of the human mind in each case, from that which is fixed and defined, to that which is eternal and infinite.

As we read the Epistle to the Romans, we are struck by this train of thought as there

[1] P. 51, &c.

opened out. First of all, in chap. ii. 14, 15, we find the apostle recognizing the voice of nature in the heathen, by which they do the things which are really enjoined by the law of God. Φύσει τὰ τοῦ νόμου ποιοῦσιν. There is after all a higher voice than the law of commandments contained in ordinances. There is a law recognized by all men, of whatsoever nation they may be. It is in the forum of conscience, and in the better sense of aggregate man, that this righteous law is discovered. So Aristotle had long ago held[1].

Writing now to Romans, the appeal to a law written in the hearts of all men, would find an echo in their ideas of a law of nature. It is this law which contains the primary principles of right and justice which the Roman saw to be common to all men. It likewise underlay the rigid rules and forms of the Mosaic code. In both cases man was pointed on to a code of exceeding high sanction, which without special revelation he felt constrained to recognize.

Thus in a larger sense than to the Jews only, the law was our schoolmaster to bring us to Christ; for now the apostle goes on to show how Christ is Himself not only the end of the law for righteousness, but how a new law of life and conduct is stepping in to accomplish

[1] Pp. 104, 105.

that which the law of Moses, equally with the law of Nature, failed to do, namely, to set men free from the law of sin and death. Thus with St. Paul the very idea of law is raised into the lofty metaphysical sphere of an abstract principle or power [1].

Here is a foundation for much after-discussion. The "jus naturale," or, as the lawyers put it, the "jus gentium and the jus naturale" in one; the lost code of nature herself, the "lex scriptum in cordibus," brings us "in foro conscientiae," to a trial, where right and wrong are to be settled; and the thought of final adjudication is projected forward "in diem," to the Day of God; unless the "in diem" be referred back to verse 12, which leaves us at any rate to hear the Divine voice in conscience.

And when we come to the law which is to supersede this one, we are reminded of the Romans' conflict between the old Quiritarian law and the Praetorian law which meted out justice on simpler principles. The readers of this Epistle would see the comparison, and grasp the teaching. While Christ had not come to destroy, but to fulfil the law of Moses in all its deeper principles, He Himself had left a higher law; a law of faith as a power and principle, and a law of sacred

---

[1] Rom. viii. 1–8.

morality which should henceforth demand a far higher standard of action than had before been known, and which should be called "the law of Christ[1]."

It will not be necessary to follow in detail every argument of St. Paul as he takes up first one idea of law and then another. From the second to the ninth chapter the apostle is reasoning with Romans, distinctly on grounds of their own, with the exception of the passage especially naming the Jew and the law of circumcision. He enters much into forensic trains of thought, as well as those relating to the Patria Potestas, inheritance, the law of marriage, &c. It is not always that these are followed out closely, but rather that they offer such apt similitudes, and supply so expressive a vocabulary, that the great principles and truths he is enunciating find an easy and felicitous expression through them.

For example, the term δικαιόω, with which we meet so often, is distinctly a Greek technical and forensic term. In iii. 4, the passage, though indeed a quotation from the Hebrew Psalter, is distinctly forensic, and falls in at once with the apostle's present line of thought. The Deity is not here regarded as a Judge, but is represented rather as a party impleaded. The de-

---

[1] Gal. vi. 2.

fendant, if cleared of blame, may well be said νικᾶν (to overcome), since he it is who carries his cause. God is shown to be, when reproving or condemning men, altogether *just*; in fact, to be vindicated even in the eyes of objectors, as to His "justum judicium."

Again, in the very next verse, the μὴ ἄδικος ὁ θεὸς ὁ ἐπιφέρων τὴν ὀργήν is spoken "after the manner of men." We may perhaps see the thought flashing back to the primitive notion of human justice and retribution, when personal wrongs were sufficient ground, under varied circumstances, for varied and extreme forms of vengeance. Is God, then, κατὰ ἄνθρωπον, unjust? "The earliest administrators of justice simulated the probable acts of persons engaged in a private quarrel. In settling the damages to be awarded, they took as their guide the measure of vengeance likely to be exacted by the aggrieved person under the circumstances of the case." The *manifest* and the *non-manifest* thief suffered very differently. The hot blood of the injured party was allowed as full play in the laws of the Twelve Tables as in many other rude codes. There may doubtless be injustice, argues the apostle, in the case of a *man*. But with the Deity not so, even though "He taketh wrath," for He "judicabit mundum [1]."

Further on, from the nineteenth verse, we are

[1] See Maine's *Ancient Law*, p. 378.

still in the forum. The whole atmosphere is law. The majesty of condemning justice sits supreme. The very "lex" heretofore spoken of finds its only place here as handing over the guilty race to the inexorable sternness of a law which is condemnation upon all. Then there arises yet another "lex," supreme over both these; the "lex fidei," which puts out of court the "lex factorum." And this law has principles of its own, so perfect and adapted, that it is vindicated by its own nature as a lex, indeed, to which the mind of one "scientis legem" cannot but agree; a law which actually triumphs in the complete justification of the criminal, and that so justly, that it re-establishes the old law which had been dishonoured.

The next chapter is much in the same spirit, having been thus prepared for, though it looks more on the Jewish side of the question, the softening light of grace and paternal love being fortified in its action by thoughts of satisfied and honoured justice.

In the fifth chapter we move into another atmosphere. Here we have what Sir Henry Maine refers to when he shows how "the nature of sin and its transmission by inheritance—the debt owed by man and its vicarious (representative) satisfaction—the necessity and sufficiency of the Atonement"—were the points which the Western or Roman Church took up with peculiar avidity [1].

The high appeal of chap. vi brings us on to another ground of law. Consistency of life is urged upon Christians, upon the soundest logic, again springing from legal principles. "He that has died is justified ($\delta\epsilon\delta\iota\kappa\alpha\iota\omega\tau\alpha\iota$) from sin." He is not only freed from it as a mortal condition, and one of servitude, *but is acquitted of its claims and penalties.* The argument is of course forensic. A glance at Scottish theology, where the juridical language of the Reformers is found to have taken root in a soil peculiarly apt, shows clearly the strength and wideness of the old jurisprudence in its influence on the conceptions of the Western mind. The late Dr. Horatius Bonar has the following remark on this passage, which he illustrates in the strictest juridical spirit: "'He that is dead is free from sin.' More correctly, 'He that has died is justified from sin.' So is, literally, the word 'freed.'" He makes the passage run: "'He that dies (and so exhausts the law's penalty and claim) is justified (or has been justified) from the sin [2].' In the terms of the old Scottish jurisprudence, 'justify' means to suffer the penalty of the law, so that a justified man would mean, one who

---

[1] *Ancient Law*, p. 357.
[2] In Roman law, it is the "Capite Minutus," discharged from all civil debts previously incurred.

had completed his term of punishment, and so was free ¹.'" Again, "Redemption forms a new obligation to law-keeping, as well as puts us in a position for it ²." Is there not here an echo of the "Obligatio ex Contractu"? Once more: "The Romish doctors and creeds ... recognize the judicial element as constituting the basis of the moral ³."

In the passage before us, moreover, the man who is dead to sin has done with it for ever, and left it as a country to which he is never to return. Do we not here see another analogy suggesting itself? In the first place to the citizen. As Christ by His death passed out of the "dominium" of the mortal state, so must His followers too, even as by the "jus postliminii" of the Romans the former condition of the citizen was absolutely suspended, and if he died without returning, was altogether annulled. By direct reasoning it is Christ who is dead to the one state, and alive beyond the border to a new and different one. By a reflection of thought it is the "lex peccati" that has lost its rights by banishment, and men are now free from its control. *Let nothing bring back that now dead dominion.* Secondly, the analogy is to the slave. The "servus" has changed his "status ⁴" by

---
[1] *Way of Peace*, p. 70.　　[2] *Ibid.* p. 150.
[3] *Way of Holiness*, p. 260.　　[4] Verses 16 23.

manumission, and is exhorted to continue in the service of perfect freedom. And the chapter winds up with a magnificent appeal to the principle so familiar to every Roman, of "legal consequence united to legal causes by an inexorable necessity, and to the 'Juris vinculum quo necessitate adstringimur alicujus solvendae rei.'"

The sanctions of the laws of marriage supply, in the seventh chapter, an apt example and a powerful argument for the Christian to live evermore as alive to Christ and dead to sin. "I speak to them that know the law," says the apostle. Here again, perhaps, there is a shadow of the "jus postliminii" in the background. The dread of a return to the dominion of sin is felt as that of a possible return to a practically dead tyrant might be, who, by the "fiction" of the law referred to, would be able to call back to life all his former rights over one who seemed to have escaped them by exile and banishment, or, by reflection of thought, by *its* exile and banishment. In the words of Justinian[1] this is explained: "If an ascendant is taken prisoner, although he becomes the slave of the enemy, yet his paternal power is only suspended, owing to the 'jus postliminii'; for captives, when they return, are restored to all their former rights. . . .

[1] *Institutes*, I. xii. 5.

The 'postliminium' supposes that the captive has never been absent. . . . So, too, if a son, or grandson, is taken prisoner, the power of the ascendant, by means of the 'jus postliminii,' is only in suspense. The term 'postliminium' is derived from 'post' and 'limen [1].'" If a captive did not return, the law considered him to have died at the moment of the commencement of his captivity.

So, in St. Paul's argument, *we* are Christ's captives, though as such now really free; consequently, we are dead to the old dominion and state of sin, though to us it appeared a condition of freedom. The reversal of the members of the analogy does not invalidate it, as see verse 6. The whole of chap. vi is an earnest entreaty to *remain and live* in the new state, and not to return to that to which we are now dead.

In chap. viii we pass into another element of Roman law. Here we are lifted into a clearer and brighter atmosphere than has yet been attained. From verse 14 to the end, the law of adoption, mentioned on p. 129, is the ground of the argument.

Not only is the word "adoption" peculiar to St. Paul in the New Testament, but the idea. The beautiful metaphor, as used by him, can

---

[1] The derivation is disputed. But Cicero gives the same derivation from Scaevola.

only be explained by reference to this great principle of Roman law[1]. In the eye of the law, the adopted person was a "new creature." He is born into a new family. The passage in Rom. viii. 14–16 is classical. Here, as elsewhere, there is the necessary witness in the ceremony of adoption. This witness is the Holy Spirit, the Third Person in the Trinity.

Let us look at the process. "The common form of adoption was singularly dramatic. It consisted of the ancient and venerated ceremonial conveyance 'with the scales and brass,' followed by a fictitious lawsuit. The proceedings took place in the presence of seven witnesses. The fictitious sale and re-sale, and the final vindication or claim, were accompanied by the utterance of legal formulae. Upon the words used depended whether the ceremony amounted to the sale of a son into slavery or his adoption into a new family. The touch of the *festuca* or ceremonial wand might be accompanied by the formula, 'I claim this man as my son,' or the formula, 'I claim this man as my slave.' The *form* of sale into bondage was almost

[1] In our own country, we use the term colloquially, and sometimes "adopt" in a free way of our own : but there is no real *law* of adoption. The same might be said, with greater force, of the Hebrew nation. With the Romans, it was an important means of the extension of the legal family. See p. 129.

indistinguishable from the *form* of adoption. It was the spirit which was different. It was the function of the witnesses to testify that the transaction was in truth the adoption of a child. The adopter it may be supposed has died: the adopted son claims the inheritance; but his claim is disputed and his status as son is denied. Litigation ensues. 'After the ceremony with the scales and brass,' declares the plaintiff, 'the deceased claimed me by the name of son. He took me to his home. I called him father and he allowed it. It is true I served him; but it was not the service of a slave, but of a child. I sat at his table, where the slaves never sat. He told me the inheritance was mine.' But the law requires corroborative evidence. One of the seven witnesses is called. 'I was present,' he says, 'at the ceremony. It was I who held the scales, and struck them with the ingot of brass. The transaction was not a sale into slavery. It was an adoption. I heard the words of the vindication, and I say this person was claimed by the deceased not as a slave, but as a son [1].'"

Does not this explain the language of St. Paul in this deeply interesting passage? "Ye have not received the spirit of bondage again to fear; but ye have received the Spirit of adoption,

[1] W. E. Ball, LL.D.

whereby we cry, Abba, Father. The Spirit itself beareth witness with [1] our spirit, that we are the children of God: and if children, then heirs."

It is not, then, that the Divine Spirit simply addresses the human spirit, as is often interpreted; it is rather that the Spirit of God and the soul of the believer both testify to the same fact.

And further to follow out this imagery. "If sons (by adoption), then heirs; heirs of God; (but more) joint-heirs with Christ" (the Son by right, and our Redeemer into sonship). The law of inheritance, consequent on adoption [2], now plays its part. St. Paul teaches men to "suffer with Christ" by the example of co-heirs. The heirship to which he refers is Roman, not Hebrew heirship. It is not necessary to wait for the father's death. The adopted son is already a participator. Besides, the personality of the father does not die. He always lives in his heirs. He is in law the same *persona* with them. The phrase, "heirs of God," is a most vivid presentation of the eternal union between the believer and his God.

Again: "Co-heirs with Christ; if so be that we suffer with Him, that we may be also glorified

---

[1] Gr. συμμαρτυρεῖν is to bear witness in accordance with another. συμμάρτυς is a "joint witness."

[2] See pp. 178, 179.

together." That is, "we must bear the charges with Him, if we would also share in the emoluments." Co-heirs, by testamentary law, accepted all the liabilities involved in the inheritance. Moreover, in Roman law all "unemancipated" children were equally successors should the father die intestate. There was no primogeniture. So with St. Paul, the heirship is joint and equal. The idea of *succession* is obviously out of place in the similitude before us, and we have before shown that the heir was reckoned such, or rather, was accounted part-possessor, even in the father's life-time. Thus the application of Roman law to the position and privileges of the Christian is full of force and instructive power.

While on this line of thought we must advert to St. Paul's Epistle to the Galatians, where the same kind of argument meets us.

Galatia itself was a Roman province. He is therefore writing to a people Celtic in race, though mixed and mingled with both Jews and Phrygians as well as Romans[1]. If St. Paul

[1] We here assume the Galatia as generally understood by Lightfoot and others.

"Galatia." In defining a new field of missionary enterprise, "the definition usually takes the form of a Roman provincial district," Ramsay, v. 1. See his remarks on "Region," Acts xiii. 49. Pisidian Antioch, a Phrygian city "towards" Pisidia, was the centre of a Roman "Regio,"

rebukes the fickleness of their character, so soon displayed in their readiness to turn back to a bondage both legal and Judaic, he earnestly endeavours to recall them to their allegiance to Christ, and to their liberty in the Gospel, by arguing with them in the legal language, not only of the Mosaic or Abrahamic covenant, but also of the legal and political system under which they lived, and which they all acknowledged.

In chap. iii. 15 he speaks "after the manner of men," and draws an illustration from their ordinary dealings with one another. Even in a human covenant or compact, once confirmed, honour and law bind the parties to faithful observance. Ὅμως ἀνθρώπου κεκυρωμένην διαθήκην οὐδεὶς ἀθετεῖ ἢ ἐπιδιατάσσεται (addeth new clauses). *A fortiori* this is true of God's covenant with man. Nor could a law (to which they "desired again to be in bondage") four hundred and thirty years later than the covenant in question, affect it so as to annul its provisions which were distinctly *not* dependent on any condition of that later law. "Wherefore then serveth the law?"—"Quid igitur Lex?"—What place has

a colony, and a military and administrative centre (v. 4). See also v. 6, "He made the limit of Roman territory the limit of his work." His guiding principle was "to go to the Roman world." See also on the Region of Galatic Lycaonia. Also vi. 1, at length.

this law, which was after all "ordinata per angelos"?

The answer is (we give the Vulgate because in our present argument it conveys so much better the suggestion of the Latin law) — "Propter transgressiones posita est." It is seen to be a kind of "pactum adjectum," only applying in its object to a certain purpose and for a certain time. At best it could only be subsidiary. So that the great "testamentum" remains paramount and eternal. And yet the intervening "lex" had its high and sacred use, and that because of the unfitness of its subjects for the enjoyment of the faith by-and-by to be revealed. So that they are now seen to have been "sub lege custodoti," and under "pedagogi" to supervise and govern them, till they were brought to their teacher Christ. But "in Christ by faith," they are now all "filii Dei;" they are "semen Abrahae, secundum promissionem heredes [1]."

[1] The Rev. G. F. Magoun, in the *Thinker* for July, 1895, questions the possibility of St. Paul's referring to the Roman law in writing to the Galatian Church, "to those ignorant of this law." Nevertheless I hold to the conviction here expressed. Even Tarsus was a "free city;" and St. Paul, though born in a district of "Greek Asia," evidently thoroughly understood his own Roman citizenship. At the same time I cannot quite go all the way with Dr. Anton Halmel, of Vienna, who in a recent pamphlet mentioned in the *Thinker* for June, 1895, has tried to show that in Gal. iii.

Having attained this point, the apostle proceeds in the next chapter on the ground of this great thought of the inheritance. He shows his readers how, under the Patria Potestas, or the "Tutela" which supplied its place, they were not free to act for themselves. But now, the "Tutela" being removed or ended, their inheritance is open to them as being fully "sui juris." Even the "haeres," as they well knew, so long as he is under age, differs nothing from a "servus" though, potentially, "sit domus omnium." So were they themselves "sub tutoribus et curatoribus," both their person and their property being under guardianship, "until the time appointed of the father." There is no reason to suppose that discretion as to the time could not be exercised under the Roman law; for Gaius says, "Si cui testamento tutor sub condicione aut ex die certo datus sit;"—and Justinian seems to assume it as a principle in the *Institutes*, I. xiv. 3—"Ad certum tempus vel

15-20, 29, there is the idea, not of covenant, but of testament. Surely here διαθήκη is used rather in the sense of *pactum*, or contract. The μεσίτης he makes a *mediator, persona interposita*; not between man and God, but between Abraham and Christ, namely Moses; that is, a mediator in *time*. Then the law is a codicil; and so on. But his object is to show that the Epistle was written in Italy, which seems quite out of the question. It is possible to strain the interpretation. But this does not invalidate a legitimate application.

ex certo tempore vel sub condicione vel ante heredis institutionem posse dari tutorem non dubitatur."

So had it been with these Christians, and in fact with all mankind. They had been in bondage under the στοιχεῖα, the elements, of the world. But now "the fullness of the time was come." The work the Son of God had come to do was one of redemption, of release from an actual condition of slavery; for "Christus nos redimit[1]," from the bondage of the "lex" under which He found us.

Once more St. Paul, in order to illustrate to the full the blessings of the Gospel dispensation, slightly changes the ground, though still proceeding on the same underlying argument from civil law. He now regards mankind as really slaves, needing redemption in order to place them in the position of sons. This is a very important and telling point. "Misit Deus Filium Suum, ut nos redimeret." He is strikingly particular here, and singularly accurate. "Ut adoptionem filiorum reciperemus." The process of sale and purchase must first take place, the "redemptio" must be complete, before the "adoptio" could really place them in the true position of "filii." There was a doubt among the ancients, though Justinian accepted the

[1] Gal. iii. 13.

opinion of Cato as decisive in the negative, as to whether an adopted slave, though made free by the adoption, acquired the rights of a son. But St. Paul will not allow this doubt to invalidate the Christian's title. Redeemed from slavery first, and then adopted, they become not "filii" alone, but undoubted "heredes" also. For the effect of adoption in the case of one who was made free, was to place the adopted exactly in the position of a son born. Thus the apostle triumphantly vindicates the liberty and the high privilege of the "filii" of the heavenly Father, whose adoption is moreover sealed in this case by sending the "Spiritum Filii Sui in corda clamantem, Abba Pater."

"Quod si filius, et haeres." There was no blot or slur on the standing of the new "filius-familias."

Thus does the apostle call in the aid of the Roman law, and profoundly reason on the deepest matters that touch mankind, in words wonderfully applicable and beautiful. These thoughts, or rather truths, have travelled down the ages, and may be as potent to the Western Christian of to-day, as they could be to the Galatian convert then; so at least they were in Luther's time, whose *Epistle to the Galatians* bears witness to the wide and catholic interpretation of which St. Paul's great argument is capable. For a similar bondage once more enslaved the "liberti," the "filii;" and the same glorious "haereditas" had to be again proclaimed to the soul of a bound and despairing Church.

At the end of this same chapter, there is an allegory of the son of the "libera" and the "ancilla." This may be drawn from the old Hebrew story, and is perfect in itself; but still the similarity and applicability of the Roman law in the same respect were perhaps also present in the apostle's mind, as he was addressing those to whom in some cases the one law would be the more familiar, to others the other. There is a remarkable passage in Titus iii. 5, where St. Paul seems to mingle the metaphor of adoption with that of the new birth: "He saved us through the washing of regeneration and renewing of the Holy Ghost, which He poured out upon us richly," &c. This was in order that "we might be made heirs according to the hope of eternal life." At any rate, such a passage from the pen of the apostle of law, shows clearly how the great spiritual facts are the same, whether described under the one phraseology or the other. We also see some foundation here for the modern expression of the doctrine of Baptismal regeneration. The symbolic act of signing with the Cross is accompanied by the words, "We receive this child into the congregation of Christ's flock." This resembles in some degree the old legal "vindication," or claim, with the "festuca," in the adoptive ceremony.

Nor is this all. The Baptismal service is cast in the form of a covenant. It actually seems to have been framed upon the pattern of the ancient Roman contract called the "stipulatio." The engagement made is from the point of view of the promisee. Certain stipulations are made, which are assented to in short answers. Besides this, the formal question and answer among the Romans might be simply, "spondes," "spondeo." So the party making the promises was called the "sponsor." The other was the "stipulator." The sponsor of course answered for himself. In Baptism the sponsors answer as though it were the baptized speaking. In adult Baptism the person is really his own sponsor; or rather, he is the sole "answerer."

Now the question and answer in Baptism are of great antiquity, being mentioned by Justin Martyr. We think at once of St. Peter's language in his first Epistle, iii. 21. In Greek the contract of "stipulatio" was known as ἐπερώτησις or ἐπερώτημα. "Baptism doth also now save us," says the apostle, συνειδήσεως ἀγαθῆς ἐπερώτημα εἰς Θεόν.

And the account of the baptism of the Ethiopian

eunuch in Acts viii. 34–38, with the "stipulation" of Philip, responded to by the answer of the eunuch, is a witness, whether the words were an after-insertion or not, of the extremely primitive nature of the practice.

The use of the metaphor of the Inheritance, as a special theological conception, is peculiarly Pauline, though the term is found in other Epistles, probably in a general Hebrew sense. But it has become the very language of the infant in the Faith, and the truth, as taught to the children of to-day, bears in its very expression the traces of the great legal system which this first messenger of the Gospel to the Gentiles did not disdain to use and sanctify[1].

Other minor references may be named. In Romans xiii the apostle deals with practical matters of everyday life. The supremacy of the Roman power furnishes apt material for inculcating the duties of citizenship, Christian neighbourliness, and obedience to "lawfully constituted authority" for the ages to come.

Even in the first Epistle to the Corinthians, so much more Greek in its character, the familiarity is perceptible of writer and readers with the laws and institutions of Rome. We find a reference to the Lictor's rod (iv. 21); to the laws of Affinity (v. 1); to the Praetor's court (vi. 1–7);

[1] See Note at the end.

application to which the apostle deprecates, suggesting instead the appointment of a "judex" of their own, who should be, as in the legal tribunal, a subordinate person, who at least might be found able to arbitrate between brethren.

Perhaps St. Paul's treatment of the matter of *slavery* exhibits more than anything else the moral force by which Christianity was to revolutionize the world. It is enough to note that the "Servus vocatus es? Non sit tibi curae: sed et si potes fieri liber, magis utere:" and the "Qui enim in Domino vocatus est servus, libertus est Domini: similiter qui liber vocatus est, servus est Christi[1]," is in entire agreement with the apostle's own action and respect for the laws as he found them with regard to the slave of Philemon, Onesimus, whom he restored to his master. The great legal system under which St. Paul lived and worked, was brought by a natural servitude to minister to Christianity. At one time to protect her messengers, at another to exhibit her principles; and again to suggest the most beautiful pleadings of Christian gentleness and affection. "Omnia sunt vestra: vos autem Christi: Christus autem Dei."

The idea of the Church, as coming from the Master, and handed on by His apostles, is not

[1] 1 Cor. vii. 21, 22.

that of a social or democratic agent; still less of a legislative panacea; but rather that of an infusion of new life into a dead and selfish world; of a leaven that shall work, in due time and according to its own laws, in the whole lump; and even this according to the reception given it by men.

Christianity, therefore, did not immediately touch the established order of the ancient world; and while teaching the equal value of the soul of the slave and of the free man, and while softening and blessing the lot of the one, and rendering more noble and brotherly the relation of the other, she left the complete revolution to work itself out in the course of centuries by the spreading of the knowledge of the great Dominus, who for us assumed "formam servi," thus rendering the bondman free with the liberty of a child of Heaven, and constraining the nobly-born of earth to own the sway and to render an absolute devotion to Him, who, as Napoleon I confessed, "across a chasm of eighteen hundred years," still "asks for the human heart;" who "demands it unconditionally; and forthwith His demand is granted."

Christianity is the "grain of mustard seed" which, taken and sown, fell into soil which had not only been prepared by the revelation of God to the Hebrew race, but enriched also by the Greek philosophy, and strengthened by the system and logic of Roman law; so that it grew, and became a great tree; "it took deep root, and filled the land, and the hills were covered with the shadow of it."

NOTE

ON THE TERMS "ADOPTION" AND "REGENERATION."

In connexion with the metaphor of adoption, which has so much coloured the theology of the Western or Latinized Church, it is important as well as interesting to note the history of the modern term "regeneration."

In Latin it is originally a botanical term, and means the transplanting of a tree, or the introduction of it into a new soil; or, the reproduction, under new conditions, of an old plant. This use is found in the elder Pliny (vii. 11. 10; xii. 1. 5), about A.D. 80. It is used also in Art, in the sense of to reproduce or resemble.

In the exactly corresponding Greek word, παλιγγενεσία, it is used for the restoration of a thing to its pristine state; e.g. the restoration of life after death; or the renewal of the earth after the Deluge. Also in the sense of the change of all things for the better; the restoration of knowledge by recollection; the restoration of righteousness which the Jews expected with the Messiah; and, cognate to this, the renewal of all things at the end of the world. The reader will do well to compare Matt. xix. 28; Titus iii. 5 (the only two passages where the actual word is used in the New Testament); Philo, i. 159; Plutarch, 2. 998. c.

In like manner, the same word is used of the admission of proselytes into the Jewish faith.

We find it also used of Cicero's restoration to his rank and fortune on his being recalled from exile (Cic. *ad Atticum*, 6. 6). Similarly, of the restoration of the Jewish nation after the exile, by Josephus (*A. J.* 11. 3, 9).

From this it may be inferred, that the term "regeneration" did not originally imply a new *nature*, but a new *condition*. It answered, when applied to the Christian religion and Christian baptism, not to a change of heart or *conversion*, but a change of relation or privilege, i. e. *adoption*. The use of it, as a change of nature, in theology, is later; perhaps due to Augustine (*Civ. Dei.* xx. 5), about 420 A.D. And this use of "regeneration" having become common in the modern Church, the doctrine of Baptismal regeneration is thought to mean Baptismal conversion, instead of Baptismal adoption, i. e. the placing a child in the family of God, under a covenant of promise, with blessings sealed and responsibilities implied [1].

---

[1] "The language of the schools is exactly that of the Latin Fathers on this point; they make the effect of baptism to be a 'regeneration,' or a 'generation to a spiritual life;' but the turning to God after a course of sin they call either 'penitence,' or 'conversion to God'" (Art. "Regeneration" in Hook's *Church Dictionary*, last edition; to the whole of which the reader is referred. See also Bp. Harold Brown, *Articles*, XXVII. i. p. 615 and note. Waterland's distinction between "regeneration" and "renovation" is noteworthy; the first being renewal (παλιγγενεσία) of the spiritual state, the second of the inward disposition).

Oxford
HORACE HART, PRINTER TO THE UNIVERSITY

PUBLICATIONS

OF THE

SOCIETY FOR

Promoting Christian Knowledge.

THE DAWN OF CIVILIZATION.
(EGYPT AND CHALDÆA.)

By Professor MASPERO. Edited by the Rev. Professor SAYCE. Translated by M. L. McCLURE. With Map and over 470 Illustrations. Demy 4to (approximately). Cloth, bevelled boards, 24s.

HISTORY OF INDIA.

From the Earliest Times to the Present Day. A New and Revised Edition. By Captain L. J. TROTTER. With eight full-page Woodcuts on toned paper, and numerous smaller Woodcuts. Post 8vo. Cloth boards, 6s.

NATURE AND HER SERVANTS;
OR, SKETCHES OF THE ANIMAL KINGDOM.

By the Rev. THEODORE WOOD. With numerous Woodcuts. Large post 8vo. Cloth boards, 5s.

ART PICTURES FROM THE OLD TESTAMENT.

Sunday Readings for the Young. A series of ninety Illustrations from original drawings by Sir F. LEIGHTON, Bart., P.R.A.; Sir E. BURNE JONES, Bart.; E. J. POYNTER, R.A.; G. F. WATTS, R.A.; E. ARMYTAGE, R.A.; F. MADOX BROWN; S. SOLOMON; HOLMAN HUNT, &c. With Letterpress Descriptions by ALEY FOX. Small 4to. Cloth boards, 6s.

BIBLE PLACES; OR, THE TOPOGRAPHY OF THE HOLY LAND.

A succinct account of all the Places, Rivers, and Mountains of the Land of Israel mentioned in the Bible, so far as they have been identified; together with their modern names and historical references. By the Rev. CANON TRISTRAM, D.D., LL.D., F.R.S. With Map. A New and Revised Edition. Crown 8vo. Cloth boards, 4s.

THE LAND OF ISRAEL.

A Journal of Travel in Palestine, undertaken with special reference to its Physical Character. By the Rev. CANON TRISTRAM, D.D., LL.D., F.R.S. Fourth edition, revised. With Maps and numerous Illustrations. Large post 8vo. Cloth boards, 10s. 6d.

THE NATURAL HISTORY OF THE BIBLE.

By the Rev. CANON TRISTRAM, D.D., LL.D., F.R.S. With numerous Woodcuts. Crown 8vo. Cloth boards, 5s.

A HISTORY OF THE JEWISH NATION.

From the Earliest Times to the Present Day. By the late E. H. PALMER, Esq., M.A. With Map of Palestine and numerous Illustrations. Crown 8vo. Cloth boards, 4s.

BRITISH BIRDS IN THEIR HAUNTS.

Being a Popular Account of the Birds which have been observed in the British Isles; their Haunts and Habits; their systematic, common, and provincial Names; together with a Synopsis of Genera; and a brief Summary of Specific Characters. By the late Rev. C. A. JOHNS, B.A., F.L.S. Post 8vo. Cloth boards, 6s.

STAR ATLAS.

Gives all the Stars from 1 to 6·5 magnitude between the North Pole and 34° South Declination, and all Nebulæ and Star Clusters which are visible in telescopes of moderate powers. Translated and adapted from the German of Dr. KLEIN, by the Rev. E. MCCLURE, M.A. New edition brought up to date. Imp. 4to. With eighteen Charts and eighty pages illustrative Letterpress. Cloth boards, 7s. 6d.

THE ART TEACHING OF THE PRIMITIVE CHURCH.
With an Index of Subjects, Historical and Emblematic. By the Rev. R. St. John Tyrwhitt. 5s.

AFRICA, SEEN THROUGH ITS EXPLORERS.
By Charles H. Eden, Esq. With Map and several Illustrations. Crown 8vo. Cloth boards, 5s.

HISTORY OF EARLY CHRISTIAN ART.
By the Rev. E. L. Cutts, D.D. Demy 8vo. Cloth boards, 6s.

AUSTRALIA'S HEROES:
Being a slight Sketch of the most prominent amongst the band of gallant men who devoted their lives and energies to the cause of Science, and the development of the Fifth Continent. By C. H. Eden, Esq. With Map. Crown 8vo. Cloth boards, 3s. 6d.

SOME HEROES OF TRAVEL;
or,
CHAPTERS FROM THE HISTORY OF GEOGRAPHICAL DISCOVERY AND ENTERPRISE.
Compiled and re-written by the late W. H. Davenport Adams, Author of "Great English Churchmen," &c. With Map. Crown 8vo. Cloth boards, 5s.

CHRISTIANS UNDER THE CRESCENT IN ASIA.
By the Rev. Edward L. Cutts, D.D., Author of "Turning Points of Church History," &c. With numerous Illustrations. Post 8vo. Cloth boards, 5s.

MAN AND HIS HANDIWORK.
By the late Rev. J. G. Wood. With about 500 Illustrations. Large post 8vo. Cloth boards, 10s. 6d.

THE FIFTH CONTINENT, WITH THE ADJACENT ISLANDS.

Being an Account of Australia, Tasmania, and New Guinea, with Statistical Information to the latest date. By C. H. EDEN, Esq. With Map. Crown 8vo. Cloth boards, 5s.

FROZEN ASIA: A SKETCH OF MODERN SIBERIA.

By CHARLES H. EDEN, Esq., Author of "Australia's Heroes," &c. With Map. Crown 8vo. Cloth boards, 5s.

HEROES OF THE ARCTIC AND THEIR ADVENTURES.

By FREDERICK WHYMPER, Esq. With Map, eight full-page and numerous small Woodcuts. Crown 8vo. Cloth boards, 2s. 6d.

CHINA.

By Professor ROBERT K. DOUGLAS, of the British Museum. With Map, and eight full-page Illustrations on toned paper, and several Vignettes. Post 8vo. Cloth boards, 5s.

RUSSIA: PAST AND PRESENT.

Adapted from the German of Lankenau and Oelnitz. By Mrs. CHESTER. With Map, and three full-page Woodcuts and Vignettes. Post 8vo. Cloth boards, 5s.

London:
NORTHUMBERLAND AVENUE, W.C.;
43, QUEEN VICTORIA STREET, E.C.

www.ingramcontent.com/pod-product-compliance
Lightning Source LLC
Chambersburg PA
CBHW020845160426
43192CB00007B/789